SPEAK THE TRUTH AND POINT TO HOPE

The Leader's Journey to Maturity

LISA J. MARSHALL

KENDALL/HUNT PUBLISHING COMPANY
4050 Westmark Drive   Dubuque, Iowa 52002

Cover Photograph by Patricia Ridenour/Getty Images

Author Photograph by Larry Wolken

Cover and Book Design by Johanna Pino

Library of Congress Catalog Card Number: 2003115062

ISBN 0-7575-0823-5

Printed in the United States of America.

For my dad,

Stan Marshall,

who read every draft
and edited, coached, inveigled
and argued me into writing
a much better book.

With gratitude, appreciation and much love.

CONTENTS

MONSTERS ⊛

METAMORPHOSIS ⊛

RETURN ⊛

EPILOGUE ⊛

FOREWORD

We need today a different kind of leadership.

In a world obsessed with effective action, we are sometimes painfully reminded that there is an even bigger challenge to master: meaningful action. Only meaningful action can lead to effective living.

It can be said that "effective action" is the turf of managers and technocrats, and "meaningful action" is the territory of leaders. We know a lot about management and effective action, but the idea of *meaningful* action brings forth some very interesting (and critical) questions and distinctions about leadership...

For example: There is, of course, nothing wrong with effective action. In fact, one of the results of leadership is effective action. In my work, I have met thousands of people attending my programs who are, by any standard, enormously effective in action. Yet many of these people express a disturbing bitterness resulting from a lack of purpose, a lack of meaning for their actions. In the end, effective action alone is insufficient. And no matter how important it may be, it is dangerous to position it as the core concern of human performance. We must look instead at what is truly meaningful action.

If, as I believe, we human beings construct reality through narratives (or stories), then leaders must be masterful storytellers and, therefore, reality builders. Leaders generate grounded narratives that "make sense" to people — in other words, they tell stories that create meaning for people. They create a context for our actions that make them meaningful. These narratives are not just mere conceptual constructions; rather, they are able to create meaning because they connect with us emotionally. The emotions they generate are the ones that predispose us to take the actions necessary to realize the world foreseen by the leader and embraced by the followers.

But the author of this book goes one step further. She says that mature leaders not only create the necessary emotional context to predispose us to the right kind of actions. They also come from, and tell stories that bring forth in us, an "unselfish, loyal, and benevolent concern for the good of another." As you will discover reading this book, this is her definition of love. And it opens another space for reflection.

All human action takes place within a context — a story, a reason for our actions, a framework that should give some meaning to what we do. Even when we act alone, we act within a context. That context may be self-centered or other-focused. One example of a self-centered context would be the current emphasis on consumerism, triggered by the seemingly fundamental human desire for "more" — a never-ending accumulation of bigger, better, more for "me."

This self-centered context creates a false sense of meaning. It looks (and — temporarily — feels) good, but it lacks substance. Its meaning is illusory, a context that will, sooner or later, evaporate and leave us searching for the next "thing" to fulfill us. Similarly, when our leaders provide us with such empty or meaningless contexts, we experience a leadership crisis. We need leaders who create greater meaning.

A genuine and meaningful action is focused outward — focused on, as mentioned earlier, "the good of another." Therefore, mature leadership not only involves service on the part of the leader, but also creates the meaningful context in which service flourishes, in which meaningful action is naturally evoked from the followers. The result is not illusory, but very real indeed.

So far in history, the concern for "the good of another" has been limited to those belonging to the "tribe" or the "nation," deeply limited by an "us vs. them" mentality. Today, with globalization, we are moving in a direction that appears to be breaking up this tribal or national mindset. Indeed, we are redefining the tribe itself. How does this affect leadership? What stories could have the power of a bigger inclusion, the power to make sense to many more people than ever before?

And what is the source of such meaningful action? What happens in the souls of those who are generating meaning, in the souls of those we call leaders? Why are they compelled to tell stories, to invent worlds, to provide direction for our actions? Why are others compelled to follow them? Is there any common ground that their dreams come from? What journey do they have to take to bring their gift to life? Why do some of them achieve mature leadership?

Throughout this book, these are not just rhetorical questions; they are concerns that show up in the many conversations that the author has with various leaders — discussing real situations in a beautiful mixture of hands-on thinking and poetic description.

With this book, Lisa Marshall has definitely written a new kind of book about mature leadership. It is an inspiring reflection on that subject, as opposed to just a list of tips for leadership development. Using the classic structure of the hero's journey, she explores the strength and turmoil of the leader's soul in a very practical manner — never losing sight of the beauty and power of all such deep human quests.

Julio Olalla
Boulder, August 25, 2003

HONOR TO THE TEACHERS

No accomplishment or understanding ever stands alone; we all stand on the shoulders of those who came before. So it is here. Honor to the teachers:

♦ Fernando Flores, Julio Olalla, Humberto Maturana, Terry Winograd, Carlos Sandoval and the other developers of Speech Acts Theory who have built on the work of J.L. Austin, John Searle and Martin Heidegger to develop the linguistic tools by which human beings can make genuine commitments to and honorable agreements with one another;

♦ Howard Gardner, Robert Sternberg, Peter Kline, Daniel Goleman and the others who, building on the work of John Dewey, have led the effort to help us understand all forms of intelligence and how to use them in designing learning;

♦ Chris Argyris, Edgar Schein, Marvin Weisbord, William Bridges, Bruce Tuckman, Eric Trist, Fred Emery and all those others who stood in turn on the shoulders of Kurt Lewin, Douglas McGregor and ultimately, Frederick Winslow Taylor in developing new ways to think about work and workplaces that let us understand the nature of groups and organizations, the power of teams and how hard it can be to see and tell the truth;

- John Grinder, Richard Bandler, Robert Dilts, Judith de Lozier, Lucy Freedman and the other developers and practitioners of NeuroLinguistic Programming (NLP) who, using the insights of Gregory Bateson, Milton Erickson, Virginia Satir and others, sought, found and made explicit the core shared behaviors of effective people everywhere;

- Robert Kegan and James Fowler and the others who have integrated the understandings of the giants of human development — Piaget, Erickson, Kohlberg and Gilligan — in ways that let us see the possibilities of emotional, intellectual, moral and spiritual maturity;

- Meg Wheatley, who took the cumulative understandings of David Bohm, Fritjof Capra, John Holland, Stuart Kauffman, Kevin Kelly, Francisco Varela, Ilya Prigogine and the others who have contributed to the development of the sciences of chaos and complexity and turned them into language that speaks to the state of organizations and human hearts today;

- David Whyte, who has sought both to preserve our souls and clarify what work can and should mean to those of us who labor in the business world, through the power of poetry and its ability to evoke the otherwise unspoken;

- Noury Al-Khaledy, Chuck Appleby, Rani Borkar, Kathy Braglia, Tony Deady, David Gaster, Kevin Kearns, Tom Rampone, Mark Shipman and Dave Tyrrell, who over the years have shared what they learned about leadership as they learned it, and graciously taught me in the process;

- And special thanks to all of the leaders who contributed to my thinking about and understanding of leadership maturity:

Noury Al-Khaledy ◆ Jane Arkus ◆ Doug Baden
Carol Bell ◆ Sue Bethanis ◆ Mary Ann Biggs
Kathy Braglia ◆ Laura Chizzali ◆ Ron Combest
Rob Crook ◆ Leah Dever ◆ Robert Dilts
Sandi Douglas ◆ Joe Dyer ◆ Lucy Fitch
Darya Funches ◆ Larry Haynes ◆ Richard Heckler
Isabelle Kaplan ◆ Kevin Kearns ◆ Dave Kelly
Liz Lerman ◆ Bob McCulloch ◆ Jim Messerschmitt
Thomas Murrin ◆ Scarlett Navarro-Robotroy
Kerry Ogden ◆ Julio Olalla ◆ Lois Oller ◆ Jody Olsen
Terry Petrzelka ◆ Glen Powell ◆ Dave Quinn
Tom Rampone ◆ Tom Rodd ◆ Deedie Runkel
Deborah Saunders ◆ Rayona Sharpnak
Mark Shipman ◆ Jane Smith ◆ Carol Stoneburner
Bill Strickland ◆ Tony Deady ◆ Lucius Theus
Dick Thornburgh ◆ Jerry Tiahrt ◆ Mike Timm
Dave Tyrrell ◆ Barbara Waugh ◆ Meg Wheatley
Warren Wilhelm ◆ Gail Williams ◆ Phil Williams
Mark Wilson ◆ Jonathan Wolken

THE SEA

The pull is so strong we will not believe
the drawing tide is meant for us,
I mean the gift, the sea,
The place where all the rivers meet.

Easy to forget,
how the great receiving depth
untamed by what we need
needs only what will flow its way.

Easy to feel so far away
and the body so old
it might not even stand the touch.

But what would that be like
feeling the tide rise
out of the numbness inside
toward the place to which we go
washing over our worries of money,
the illusion of being ahead,
the grief of being behind,
our limbs young
rising from such a depth?

What would that be like
even in this century
driving toward work with the others,
moving down the roads
among the thousands swimming upstream,
as if growing toward arrival,
feeling the currents of the great desire,
carry time toward tomorrow?

Tomorrow seen today, for itself,
the sea where all the rivers meet, unbound,
unbroken for a thousand miles, the surface
of a great silence, the movement of a moment
left completely to itself, to find ourselves adrift,
safe in our unknowing, our very own,
our great tide, our great receiving, our
wordless, fiery, unspoken,
hardly remembered, gift of true longing.

~ DAVID WHYTE[1]

Allergic to poetry? I expect many of my readers will be. Nonetheless, I begin this book with a poem. The poet David Whyte is a man who is clear about his call — bringing poetry with us into the twenty-first century. Only poetry, he says, will help us develop language to understand this strange new world we are in. Only poets will give us words "commensurate with what we're experiencing," both as leaders and as followers.

I first read this poem just as I was beginning to write this book. I was wrestling with the question of what moves people into taking the risks and enduring the pain that leadership often entails. "Why do it?" I wondered. Then I ran across his phrase, "the gift of true longing," and thought "That's why! It's that gift of true longing for something better, bigger, more beautiful, that all leaders share, whether they are the kind who *have* to lead or they are the reluctant leaders."

Later, as I was well into the writing, I happened to reread the poem, and was struck by the realization that, although it is not ostensibly a poem about leadership, there were other phrases in it that captured key elements of what I was talking about. I used those phrases as chapter titles. Read the book, and then read the poem again. See if it does not somehow speak to you of the kinds of primal forces that stir us into leadership.

PREFACE

We begin with a story:

The Preparation

I have been fascinated for a long time by two things: leadership and stories.

I taught communication and collaboration skills in corporate environments, and I met a lot of people who were called leaders. Some of these people deserved the title, but most of them did not, though they may have been gifted managers. I worked with those managers for years, helping them manage better and largely ignoring the leadership issue.

After a while, it was clear that some of the companies for which I worked were not doing well. Every person and organization has a story, the explanations they give themselves about who they are, where they are going, and why. While these clients of mine were powerful companies that had started industries, the stories they told about themselves no longer worked. Their old stories were dying, and the manager/leaders in those companies were not coming up with compelling new ones.

Here and there, however, I saw leaders who did invent new stories, at least for the people with whom they worked. Observing them, I realized the power that came from being purposeful about one's stories. So when my clients complained about the lack of a clear and compelling vision and its consequences, such as muddled decision-making and lack of focus, I said "Well, if your bosses won't give you a story, make one up! What do you have to lose? So what if they make you change it in six months? That was going to happen anyway, and you might get some traction in the meantime."

"Well, okay, how do we do that?" they asked. In one of my better moments, I decided to use a framework for story-building called the hero's journey. The scholar Joseph Campbell identified this format as the fundamental architecture of truly great stories. I began helping clients create stories their people would want to be part of, stories that opened a compelling future for their organizations.

These leaders enjoyed such good results from their intentional story-building that I thought I should write a book about it. While there is a growing body of literature about stories and story-telling, few books offer a personal roadmap for developing one's own great story. I envisioned a book that would help more people understand the structure of a great story and how to build stories that mattered and had impact.

The Call

As I got into the writing, however, I realized there was a deeper issue to be addressed. Many of these organizations were suffering not only because their old stories had died, but because the quality of their leadership had deteriorated in parallel to the quality of the stories people in those organizations held about the nature of leadership. At least since the 1960s, most of our popular stories about leadership have been variations on the theme of Peter Pan — the charismatic boy leader who always plays and never has to grow up and experience the consequences of his choices. Michael Milliken of junk bonds fame, Steve Case of AOL, Michael Armstrong of AT&T, Larry Ellison of Oracle all come to mind as examples, as do most of the dot-com-era CEOs. Such a story about leadership does not hold either the power or the profound moral center needed for the world in which we are now living.

So I began my own journey. At first, I wondered if I should focus on specific categories of leadership. There are so many — business, political, sports, scientific, cultural, religious, intellectual, people who lead from the front of the room, people who lead from the back of the room. I realized that I wanted to focus on the essence of leadership, on what could be said about all forms of great leadership, in all places, at all times. I also realized that I did not equate leadership with power — nor with management — though a relationship obviously exists. Many people with power are not leaders and there are leaders like the Dalai Lama who have no visible source of power.

I was first exposed to Joseph Campbell's work on stories through Bill Moyer's PBS series, *The Power of Myth*, in the 1980s. Campbell claimed that the great stories, the great epics, all had the same underlying structure. There was always a journey to be taken, an exploration of the unknown. Within the journey, there was always a call to action, a reason the hero or heroes had to leave the familiar and venture into that unknown. Along the way, the heroes inevitably did what Campbell called "falling into the pit." To escape the pit they would have to successfully face some kind of monster, undergoing a metamorphosis to conquer their fears. Often there were many experiences of the pit along the journey. Eventually, or periodically, the heroes would return home, appearing to be the same in some ways but different in many others, having learned and grown throughout the journey.

Campbell observed that many cultures built three phases of this archetypal pattern of human experiences into their rituals and traditions. The preparation phase was the education of children up to the point of physical adulthood. The journey commenced with physical adulthood, but required experiencing the pit through intense, often frightening ritual encounters, such as killing a lion, to be accepted as an adult into the community. And ultimately, there would be the return, coming back to the familiar, but in a more adult, mature way, fit to eventually become a member of the council of elders.

The Pit

As I started to write Chapter VI, I asked myself: "What is the point of the journey? Why do we have to take a journey? And why is it that so often we start the journey intending to somehow change the world, yet we rarely do, but instead change ourselves?" I could only think of one answer: the actual point of the journey was to grow up, to mature. We must gain not just knowledge, but wisdom. Ultimately, the goal is to become a wise elder.

By maturing, I mean the term as the late Rabbi Edwin Friedman used it: "the willingness to take responsibility for one's own emotional being and destiny."[3] The mature person, he says, is:

> Someone who has clarity about his or her own life goals, and, therefore, someone who is less likely to become lost in the anxious emotional processes swirling about ... I mean someone who can manage his or her own reactivity to the automatic reactivity of others, and therefore be able to take stands at the risk of displeasing.[4]

The mature leader, he says, is "the one who can express him- or herself with the least amount of blaming and the one who has the greatest capacity to take responsibility for his or her own emotional being and destiny."[5]

Since this was to be a book about leadership, I began by researching the literature on leadership maturity, but found that, other than Friedman's posthumously published (and unfinished) book, there was very little to explore. Most of the many books I read on leadership consisted of one or two chapters that listed leadership attributes (behaviors leading to meaningful action) and nine chapters on management (behaviors leading to effective action). As the leadership attributes seemed to fit Hitler and Gandhi equally well, such lists did not strike me as terribly useful. They certainly did not answer the questions I had about grown-up leadership.

For the most part, the assumption seemed to be that leadership capability was kind of a preset switching mechanism; either your switch was set to "on" or it wasn't. No one asked why or how that switch was activated. And even the books that purported to discuss leadership development never offered a maturity model, or described any kind of developmental progression that a thoughtful leader could expect to experience. I assumed I was just missing the real stuff and kept reading and asking colleagues in the field until I realized: *there was almost no literature to be found on leadership maturity.*

In fact, while there is enormous attention paid to leadership development, we have almost no public conversation in our society about the end point — mature, "developed" leadership. Perhaps this is because, as one publisher told me, "*Everyone* who writes a book about leadership thinks it's a book about leadership maturity, even if they don't call it that." Or perhaps it is because, as a culture, we in the United States do not know much about, let alone have positive associations with anything having to do with getting older. We certainly do not want to talk about it.

At that point, this book took a ninety-degree turn. I needed to talk to real leaders. I asked friends and colleagues to name people who, if they called tomorrow and said "I need you; come work with me," that request would be irresistible. (That seemed to me to capture the essence of what we experience in a leader.) I had conversations with over fifty of those nominated: CEOs and people in mid-level positions, school superintendents, dance troupe founders, sergeants, admirals, generals, non-profit directors, government agency heads, governors, judges, street gang leaders and many of the leaders in my own field of organizational and personal change.

I talked with these people about leadership and about growing up. We explored definitions and sources of leadership and what they thought was its source. I asked them why people are driven to lead and how we recognize leadership in ourselves or in others. They described their leadership journeys and their thoughts about the journey and the destination. I asked them to describe the ways in which they felt they had grown up, and the ways they had not. These were grand and glorious conversations!

I also began to immerse myself in developmental psychology, as well as in the work of people who had looked at moral and spiritual development. The question of whether I could create a developmental model loomed large for me. Who was I to try such a thing? Then I realized that a) it would be a lot easier to start the conversations about leadership maturity if there were a model, b) that model didn't have to be perfect and c) I was the one asking the question, so why not try to formulate an answer? I was completely in over my head — what a marvel! I went back to writing.

The Monster

What I discerned through these conversations is that, at the heart of mature leadership, the kind of leadership we need these days, is love. Love of life, love of one's work, love of truth, love of learning and love for other people. Love that is daily demonstrated in people's willingness to tell the truth as they see it and still find the hope in the situation.

It does not mean leadership is some sort of superhuman feat. Those kinds of love are practiced every day by literally hundreds upon thousands of people all over the world, people just like you and me. They are the ones who have accessed the power of loving their work and loving the people with whom they work as well. Despite this, it seems almost taboo to talk about love and leadership in the same sentence. Yet that may be precisely the shift that needs to take place.

Metamorphosis: What's Love Got to Do With It?

"Why aren't you focusing on the hard stuff, like truth-telling or integrity, the messages our leaders really need to hear today?" "Nobody wants to hear about love." "You're on dangerous ground here if you want your book to be read," people repeatedly warned me as I worked on the book. "You may be right, but you can't talk about love in this organization."

Yes, it is dangerous ground. If we learned to recognize that love was at the core of mature leadership, leadership that is generous and generative, forgiving and disciplined, leadership that creates the worlds we secretly yearn for, we would indeed pose problems. Because we would not settle for the leadership we currently have.

We would ask our leaders to ask *us* the hard questions. We would ask our leaders to invite us into the conversations where meaning gets made and value established. We would know that the famous leaders are rarely the great leaders. We would know that the way we recognize the mature leaders is through the way they make us feel and act; bigger, stronger, more generous, competent, capable and committed to our own highest values.

We would also know that "the bottom line" is merely a metaphor for a yearning for greatness, and that companies don't exist merely to make money any more than human beings exist merely to make blood. People can't live without making blood, and companies can't exist without making money, but their purpose is always something larger.

So if love is a major part of leadership, what is "love"? The dictionary offers this definition of love as a noun amongst others: "unselfish loyal and benevolent concern for the good of another." As a verb, it also means "to thrive." Its roots are in Old English and Germanic words that mean "to esteem and trust," as well as "belief and faith."

Here is how I define love in the workplace: it is a deeply felt caring for the work we do and the people we do it with, a zest for the life we are leading and a passion for the world in which we are doing it. This love is not soft and fuzzy. It is rigorous and demanding and unwilling to be "nice" when tough kindness is required. It sets high expectations and then offers the support that enables people to meet them.

This love *requires* truth and integrity. It asks us to grow up, let go of our egos, learn to know when to hold our boundaries and when to fold them. This love asks us to ask the bigger questions — is this just good for me or is it good for the team, the division, the organization, the community, the planet? It is this love that gets us to step back and look at a situation and ask, "Is this not only legal, but the right thing to do ethically, morally?"

Why then is love so unspeakable? Maybe because we use that one word in English to mean so many different things. Possibly because the workplace, frankly, is designed to be a manly place, and real men don't talk about love. Probably because we have so deeply subscribed to the "rational man" view of economics, to Frederick Winslow Taylor's view of the workplace, a place where everything should be deconstructed to its smallest possible part and then reassembled, and to the machine metaphor of work, that we do not see room for love in those models.

But I would submit that, ultimately, we do not talk about love and leadership together because *the* hardest thing in life is to learn to act with love instead of jealousy (aka competitiveness), ego, fear and greed (aka fear of scarcity). We are so afraid we will not measure up that we blind ourselves to the loss and shut the conversation off.

Yet the hard, cold truth is that the only community most of us have these days is our workplace. If we do not find and give love in our workplace, we starve emotionally. It is not enough (though enormously important) to go home to a loving family at night and on the weekends. For most people, the reality is that the best part of their waking life is spent at work. If their hearts are not used and nourished there, how will they have anything left to give when they get home?

The Return

I am still fascinated by the power of organizational stories to set courses and motivate organizations, but I have become more and more clear that the stories we currently hold about leadership are primarily stories of leadership without love — and they are woefully inadequate to the job at hand. Leadership in every field today must result in far better solutions than we currently have.

Recent research correlates the likelihood of armed conflict and population age-bulges; the younger the male population, the greater the likelihood of war.[6] Clearly youthful energy will find outlets, and we do not yet know how to channel that energy. Biological aging, however, does not necessarily equate to or guarantee wisdom or peaceability.

For example, many Baby Boomers, the generation that currently should be modeling maturity, appear to think it is acceptable to behave like greedy children. When Dick Brown, the former CEO of Electronic Data Systems (EDS), a leading, publicly traded computer services company, proclaimed in a corporate town hall that because he has an expensive wife, it was okay for him to get a bonus when the company did not make its numbers and no other employees were rewarded,[7] EDS was not experiencing mature leadership.

Such a profound lack of leadership costs us in every way, including in our hearts and souls. I believe the lack of mature leadership now will cost our children and grandchildren even more dearly. It's time to talk about leaders who grow up and practice a very old, yet seemingly very new form of leadership.

My goal is therefore to jump-start a new conversation about leadership. I will have succeeded if this book annoys, provokes, inspires *or* delights you, as long as you go out and talk to someone else about the ideas you discover here.

First Consumer Protection Warning: Who Should NOT Read This Book

It is customary in prefaces to list the kinds of people who will benefit from reading the book. Upon reflection, I found it simpler and more straightforward to identify the people who should *not* bother to read this book:

- Anyone who thinks that the current state of leadership — in business, in the public sector, in our faith communities, in education or in international affairs — is just fine;
- Anyone who thinks leadership and management are the same thing;
- Anyone looking for a quick fix or seven steps to instant leadership;
- Anyone who thinks that everything there is to say about leadership has already been said;
- Anyone who thinks that stories are a waste of time;
- Anyone who thinks he or she does not have time to think deeply about love, maturity, trust, humility, clarity, compassion, values and the spiritual self in relationship to his or her leadership.

If, however, you have sensed that the leadership training you attended missed the point, or have yearned for a deeper conversation about leadership, or have wanted, as a leader, to see more integrity and clearer standards in the people who were leading *you*, then this book is likely to speak to your condition. And if you have ever been in a position of responsibility and found yourself wondering when the grownups were going to show up, or you longed to work for someone who made you feel terrific about yourself *and* held you to high standards, then you will find this provocative reading.

Second Consumer Protection Warning: What You Can Expect

This is *not* a story about leadership as commonly practiced today. The way many leaders currently behave does not meet our needs, let alone the needs of tomorrow. Nor is this a book about management. (Managers get things done through positional power.) This is a book about genuine and mature leadership, leaders who engage people and consciously elicit their commitment without needing scapegoats.

Much of what has been said about leadership can fit a wide range of people, from the great humanitarian leaders to the truly horrific tyrants. This book calls for a clear form of leadership maturity, a deeply ethical leadership that avoids blaming others, fearmongering or intimidation. Instead, it consistently evokes the best and biggest in people's hearts and souls, so as to enable them to reach higher order solutions in every arena — economic, environmental, political and social — than any we have currently developed.

Speak the Truth and Point to Hope is less a book about how to *do* leaderly things than it is an exploration of a way of *being*, a *leaderly* way of being. It is a study of the leadership required if human beings are to remain a viable species.

Does that sound extreme? In a world inhabited by six billion people, where it frequently seems that there are as many armed conflicts as there are countries, in a world where mega-businesses spring up and die off in less than ten years, in a world where economic success and ecological catastrophe often go hand in hand and threaten to poison (or bankrupt) the planet on which we and our children have to live, such leadership is not a trivial concern. We are being called to invent new forms and new ways of leading. Or perhaps rediscover very old ones. If such things do not interest you, read no further.

About the Title

A few days after September 11, 2001, National Public Radio broadcast a piece on a woman named Jacquie Maughan, the founder and director of Pacific Crest School, a Montessori school in Seattle, and how the school was handling recent events. In the piece, Maughan was quoted as believing that the leader's role is to "speak the truth and point toward hope." A colleague of mine heard the piece and relayed the phrase to me. Over the ensuing months, I became more and more enamored of that phrase, sensing how deeply it captured the essence of the kind of leadership that the twenty-first century will require of all of us.

The Reader's Path

The diagram on the following page illustrates the spiral nature of the leader's journey and hence illustrates the reader's path through *Speak the Truth and Point to Hope*. It also provides a "locator" diagram, a way of checking where you are on the journey throughout the book. If you'll check the Table of Contents, you'll see that each section has its own version of this symbol, which is also found at the bottom of all the right-hand pages for that section, to help you remember where you are.

The journey is as follows: after a time of preparation, the leader receives a call to action. Embarking on his journey, the leader enters the pit. But in order to escape the pit, he must first face his monsters, and in so doing achieve a metamorphosis. When the change is complete, he returns home, changed yet the same in his essence, until the next call begins the process again.

THE LEADER'S JOURNEY TO MATURITY

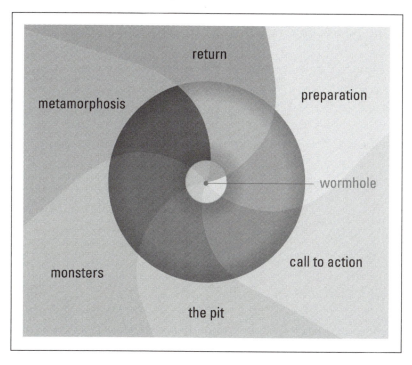

The structure of this book follows that same path. The preparation begins with an exploration of some of the definitions of leadership that emerged in my fifty-plus leadership conversations. (A copy of the questions used for those conversations appears in Appendix B.)

I also introduce the concept of the living story — the one we're in right now — and address the notion of being the hero in your own story. I discuss how to discover your living story. I examine the stories we collectively hold about leadership itself and consider what role elderhood might have to play. I introduce the concept of "wormholes" (key "inflection points," as Andy Grove, founder of

Intel, calls them), the dramatic transitions of the journey, where one finds oneself abruptly changed in some profound way.

Then I describe the first wormhole, the call to leadership — what does it mean to be called to lead? Why do we do it? I explore the notion of the hero, look at the many archetypal roles heroes can play and point out that nobody leads alone.

Following the call is the inevitable fall into the pit. To escape the pit, the leader must face the monsters; this is perhaps the most important and most difficult step on the journey. I discuss the nature of the monsters inevitably encountered on our journeys. Even though these monsters may seem to be external people or events, ultimately, that is rarely the case. Most often, the monsters are you and I — how we respond to those people or events. I highlight the developmental tension between our need for autonomy and our need for connection. It is this tension that drives how we define monsters and how we respond to them. I delve into the implications of that developmental process for leadership.

In the discussion about facing monsters, I explore the nature of maturity in each of four critical domains: intellectual, emotional, moral and spiritual. I identify the likely monsters in each domain. The reader begins to see how with mature leadership, the focus inevitably shifts from doing to being, from action to essence.

Ultimately, those two qualities merge, and mature leaders do much of their doing by their being. They influence, enable and help discern the meaning in the moment, helping make clear where value lies in the situation. They enlarge those around them so that others feel more competent and committed.

In the chapter on metamorphosis, I explore in depth the wormhole concept, the deep change experience. I identify four frequently reported wormholes and discover their implications for leadership maturity.

Campbell notes that, in the truly great stories, when the heroes return home, those heroes are the same but they are also different — changed by their experiences. What does that mean for leadership development? To what does one return? How is one the same, and how has one changed? And what does one then give back? Does fear of aging have anything to do with the refusal to address leadership maturity? All these questions are addressed in the last chapter.

After certain chapters, I've included a leadership conversation from my research. Those far-ranging conversations vastly illuminated my thinking about leadership and my spirit and provided me with much of the best language used in this book. Those leaders and I did not always agree, as you will see, but the conversations mutually expanded our thinking considerably. I'm honored and grateful to the people who gave so much of their time and thoughtful attention.

You may want to wait and read the interviews separately, so as not to interrupt your own flow of ideas, or you may want to read them as they occur, as each is designed to amplify and/or provide a counterpoint to the ideas in the chapter they follow. Either way, I know you will find their contributions a rich addition to the conversation we are starting here.

PREPARATION

I | THE WHO OF LEADERSHIP

*The person who influences me the most
is not he who does great deeds
but he who makes me feel I can do great deeds.*

~ MARY PARKER FOLLET, 1918[8]

The stories we tell ourselves about leadership are a great part of our preparation, the groundwork that is laid before our journey begins. Those stories have much to do with what we believe our possibilities to be. For example, if only "great" people can be leaders, then most of us are less likely to recognize that leadership is within our grasp. If, on the other hand, anyone can lead in the right time and place, then, if and when we see the need, perhaps you and I will take our turn as leaders. Or, if our story is that leadership emerges as needed in a given situation, then we will trust that all have a part to play and leadership will emerge, as anticipated.

Similarly, if leadership is a quality a person either has or does not have, it is difficult to see how such qualities can grow and be developed in each of us. If someone has those qualities, that person is complete, with no need to develop further. Or our story may be that a given leader has a chance to grow much further, that his or her journey has just begun. Many of us might mistakenly believe that we should never be seen as a follower, not understanding that mature leaders also know how to follow.[9] In every case, the stories set the frame for what is possible.

Leading Questions

So, what are the qualities that invite or compel one person to follow another? How does the "leader" demonstrate she has the right stuff, the ability to envision a way forward, the conviction that an idea will work and that ineffable quality that invites others to trust her judgment? What causes a person to step up and say, "This needs to be done and I will do it?" Do leaders have to have followers before they lead, or do they simply do what must be done and discover their followers in the process? Is leadership always a function of that special grace called "charisma"? These are some of the questions to be considered in this book. Fundamentally, they are all questions about the story in our minds and hearts about leadership today.

Joseph Campbell, the scholar of mythology, described a fundamental architecture that all the great stories had in common, whether they came from Asia, Europe, Africa or the Americas. The common elements (a time of preparation, a call to action, heroes, a journey, a pit, monsters, a metamorphosis and a return to home) lead one to wonder: what *is* the leader's call to action, especially now, at the beginning of the twenty-first century? What is the real nature of heroism for women and men in this complex, fast-paced and networked world? What is the developmental path, the leadership journey, likely to be? What are the natures of the monsters encountered on such a journey? How and when does one return home? How is one the same and yet different? At another level, what should one return, or give back? As one seeks to identify the qualities and forms of leadership that the twenty-first century will require, these are questions that must be answered.

Who Leads?

Leading has been defined many times, in many ways, all of them undoubtedly useful in a given context. Yet, ultimately, separating the "what" of leading from the "who," separating what people do from what their character is, seems useless. As one young leader observed,

> It's difficult to separate leadership from the leader — it comes from someone having a personal stake in what goes on, what needs to happen, the fate of the organization or

the project. Good leaders put their whole selves into it, so separating them from their attributes is difficult.[10]

For our purposes, we will look at the "what and who" of leadership as a dynamic, interactive set of relationships — relationships to people and relationships to circumstances. Within those relationships, effective, ethical and positive leadership has the following qualities:

- **Leaders sense possibility.** "A leader is someone who thinks for, listens for and evokes action on behalf of a compelling future."[11] To show the way by going first, leaders "create stories to which other people want to belong."[12] Then they hold those stories, becoming the story keepers. This means keeping the boundaries clear about what is in and what is *not* in the story. Hewlett-Packard (HP), for its first fifty years, held a story that said the company existed to further the field of engineering. Based on that, HP's leaders walked away from many short-term market opportunities they believed did not contribute to the field of engineering.

  That ability to clearly delineate the boundaries and to consistently act based on clear priorities ensures that people can make sense of current circumstances and are free to concentrate on what really matters in light of the story they are living. Such stories invite people to enact their own journeys in service to the larger story. In other words, through sensing possibility and telling its story, leaders *create a sense of time and space for great work to get done.*

- **Leaders are accountable.** Leaders take responsibility. They have the willingness to stand up and say, "This needs to happen and I will make it so." They show the way and enroll others in achieving the story. Part of that responsibility includes the willingness and ability to *contain anxiety*, to hold theirs internally without spreading it. The leader's confidence in him-

or herself, in the people on the team and the importance of the story, in the project or other shared outcome is critical. It creates a psychological and moral boundary that keeps fear and anxiety at bay.

In bearing responsibility, the leader protects the team from personal doubts and anxieties, as well as the doubts and anxieties of others in the organization or in the larger world. When Gene Krantz at NASA announced "There will be no failure on my watch" during the Apollo 13 shuttle crisis, he set a boundary in place that freed people from their anxiety and allowed them to concentrate wholly on the task at hand — bringing the astronauts safely home.

◆ **Leaders are connected**. Leaders engage in dialogue and deep listening. They make sure that *the right conversations* happen with the right people, so that action is continuously coordinated and results achieved. Initially, this listening is focused inside the leader, then inside the organization or community as people go through the stages of group development, so that people can commit to clear outcomes and learn to manage the boundaries themselves.

Over time, the leader's focus shifts to the external world, listening and creating the connections that support what needs to happen in the bigger scheme of things. Ultimately, the focus of that listening is on stewardship, the responsibilities of the leader and the leader's organization to the community, the greater good, that includes economic, ecological, social, religious and political concerns.

In 1997, Brian Brink, Senior Vice President for Medical Services at Anglo American, South Africa's most powerful company, wrote bluntly to the company's top executives, describing the implications of South Africa's sky-rocketing rate of AIDS infection: "If you look at the socioeconomic impact of that, you start recognizing this as a disaster. It's not business as usual. You can't stand back and watch. You have to lead," noted Brink.[13] Today Anglo is providing AIDS drugs to its employees. That is stewardship.

What Do Leaders Do?

How, then, do leaders behave differently from others? What exactly makes one person's behavior "leadership" and another person's behavior not leadership? This is a subtle question, one that has been asked ever since the inception of leadership. The answers are both fascinating and elusive. Offered here for consideration are three fundamental leadership behaviors:

♦ **Leaders set moods.** Moods are emotional states. It is impossible for any person not to be in a mood. Further, moods are infectious. Leaders understand some moods are productive, some moods are passive and some moods prevent work from being done. For example, optimism as a mood energizes people and increases productivity, while anxiety as a mood impairs work and can ultimately settle into cynicism. The most corrosive mood any organization, group or community can have is cynicism. Cynicism pretends a proactive response to fear or despair, but is ultimately a failure of courage that destroys innovation, creativity and vitality as surely as night follows day. A cynical organization, while it may be extremely competent, cannot do great work, because it has abdicated responsibility for the results it creates. (Nor can a cynical community raise healthy children.)

Leaders detect and shift moods from cynicism and despair to hope and possibility. Mature leaders do this without demonizing others or creating scapegoats along the way. Franklin Roosevelt's "The only thing we have to fear is fear itself" during the dark days of the Depression was mood management without scapegoating at its finest.

- **Leaders tell the stories.** Specifically, leaders make and hold meaning by telling stories of possibility that also encompass the truth of current reality. Embedded in those stories are strategy and long-range vision, told in a comprehensive hero's journey in which everyone in the organization can imagine themselves. (A strategic plan may not sound like a story, but a good one has all the same elements.[14]) Such a story guides people's actions and influences their choices as they proceed with business. It sets the organization's (or a nation's) compass for "true north," so that, whatever the current economic or political terrain, people know the right direction to head, how to behave and what constitutes taking care of the tribe.

At the same time, the story identifies the monsters that must be faced, those dragons that have to be effectively encountered so the hero can return home triumphant. In doing so, the story makes meaningful the work people have done or will do, assigns value to their efforts and recognizes their contributions to a greater good. Winston Churchill's famous "We shall fight on the beaches, we shall fight on the landing grounds, we shall fight in the fields and in the streets, we shall fight in the hills; we shall never surrender," is a good example of such a story.

- **Leaders control their own behavior.** Leaders are sensitive to context,[15] yet remain consistent in their behavior. They are also capable of deep and compassionate listening, both inside and outside the organization. Leaders balance what they hear from their customers (and their customers' customers) or constituents with what they hear from people in their organization about capability and passion.

Leaders embody their stories, so there is consistency between words and actions. They hold the connection between organizational intention and structure, between what is desired and what is measured. Leaders set the boundaries and manage the context so that people are allowed to focus on their work.

Clara Barton, founder of the American Red Cross, illustrates this capacity to manage multiple contexts while remaining consistent in her behavior. Through caring for her injured brother as an eleven- and twelve-year-old and teaching school for 18 years, her gifts for caring and educating were developed. When the Civil War started, she organized a relief program for soldiers that earned her the nickname "Angel of the Battlefield." She also started a program to locate missing soldiers.

Exhausted by her work, in 1869 she traveled to Europe to recuperate, but found herself instead in the Franco-Prussian conflict. Here she first saw the International Red Cross in action. She came home determined to have the United States sign the Geneva Convention, which it did in 1882, making the work of the American Red Cross possible. She rewrote the Red Cross constitution to expand its service to disaster relief in peacetime, and headed up many American relief efforts, finally resigning her post at the age of 82. Clearly Barton held a consistent story throughout her life time: "You must never so much as think whether you like it or not, whether it is bearable or not; you must never think of anything except the need, and how to meet it."[16]

None of the behaviors I have listed is a function of positional power. It is the rare individual who develops both the capability to lead and the capability to manage. During periods of sustained growth, managerial behaviors, such as technical competence and reliability of results, are the traits leading to promotion in most organizations.

Similarly, it has often been noted that managerial skills lead to promotion in peacetime military establishments. Leaders — people who practice the behaviors just described — may get promoted as well; then again, they may get punished. The requirements of management — control and measurement — lend themselves to playing games with fundamental leadership issues like accountability. It is one reason our organizations and communities are in such trouble today.

At the end of the day, however, people follow hearts more than heads. We are not moved by little visions or small stories. Logic alone does not provide meaning or the vehicle for sense-making. We follow big stories, passion, commitment, a sense of powerful possibility, especially if they are aligned with sound analysis and models. Only when story and behavior are in sync, when form, function and behavior align, do you get a galvanized, aligned community or organization that can complete its hero's journey and make its story one of triumph, complete with integrity, truth, compassion and love.

Conclusion: We Need a Bigger Story

The stories told today about leadership — its nature, its impact, how it works and what is required of leaders — simply are not big enough for the times we live in. New levels of stewardship and responsibility, bigger-picture thinking and more encompassing hearts are needed by twenty-first century leaders. That will not happen without building a story about leadership that invites great wisdom and maturity, as well as a deep capacity for love and compassion. Leaders are needed whose hearts and minds are big enough for the job.

II | WHY STORIES?

> *"I would ask you to remember only this one thing," said Badger. "The stories people tell have a way of taking care of them. If stories come to you, care for them. And learn to give them away where they are needed. Sometimes a person needs a story more than food to stay alive. That is why we put these stories in each other's memory. This is how people care for themselves."*
>
> ~ BARRY LOPEZ, *Crow and Weasel*[17]

Before human beings settled onto farms and began lives of relative predictability, they gathered at night around campfires and told stories. Through those stories they learned from one another. They learned the signs that might tell them where the animals lived, they learned of places where roots and tubers might grow, they learned where fresh water was to be found and where honey bees hid.

And they learned, most importantly, of triumph through courage or cunning, of sacrifices made by parents for children, of the power of love and of overcoming fear. A story well-timed and well-told offers powerful vicarious learning, the next best thing to firsthand experience. (In some instances where the experience could be life-threatening a story may be the best thing.) From stories, children learned to "imagine a course of action, imagine its effects on others and decide whether or not to do it."[18] They learned of learning, of gaining greater understanding. They learned what behavior benefited the tribe and what behavior endangered it. They learned of the past and learned for the future. Through stories, children were prepared for their lives.

In the process, the human brain became hardwired for holding complex information in story form and for learning through stories.

Stories operate as much in one's emotional (mammalian) brain as in one's thinking (neo-cortical) brain. When people hear the words, "I'm going to tell you a story," they relax, they open up. They listen in a special kind of way. They become receptive to new information and new possibilities. The result of that state is that people retain more of what they hear. They internalize it and convert it to usable information more effectively.

In a *Harvard Business Review* article on "Strategic Stories," the authors note that "A good story (and a good strategic plan) defines relationships, a sequence of events, cause and effect and a priority among items — and those elements are likely to be remembered as a complex whole."[19] Stories create pathways, help us make decisions.

In other words, stories are how we make meaning. Human beings are meaning-making creatures. In the absence of information or a shared story, humans fill in gaps with personal assumptions and create a story. Think how quickly rumors spread and then get told with increasing authority (and decreasing accuracy). As Jeanie Duck observes in her book *The Change Monster*:

> Too often leaders are so wrapped up in the issues of running the business they fail to recognize the importance of communication; they say too little and often say it too late. One thing you should count on: *people will connect the dots in the most pathological way possible.* In the absence of communication from the leaders, the organization will seek information from other sources, whether those sources know what they're talking about or not. Your silence doesn't stop the conversation; it means you're not participating in it.[20]

Have you ever noticed how two people can attend the same meeting and make very different reports? Mood, past experience, culture, gender, beliefs — these are just some of the filters through which people sift data and select their story. This filtering process exists collectively in organizations as well. What we pay attention to shapes the stories we tell. And the stories we have been told shape what we pay attention to.

Another reason that stories are important is that they are the means by which our language becomes action. A story not only expresses motivation, it motivates. It not only describes learning, it embodies, reflects and causes learning. Telling the story over and over makes it real. As the group's story evolves and grows, it becomes a vehicle through which the group can act "as if" and bring new ideas and worlds into being.

It is also a form of learning shared with a community, which again results in individuals becoming more than they believed possible. Each person has a story, the one being lived right now, his or her living story. The work done with others becomes a living story as well; the ability to recognize and articulate that larger living story — often transparent to those who are living in it — is part of the great gift a leader brings the rest of us.

Stories and Leadership

We build our identities through the stories we tell — the ways we represent ourselves to the world externally and internally. In this sense, stories are a self-fulfilling prophecy; believing the story drives behavior and so creates a reality that reinforces it. Thus, stories have enormous power over who we think we are, what we believe can be accomplished and how much hope we hold for having impact on life. When we have listened deeply to the living stories around us and fashioned them into a larger composite living story that we then tell compellingly, we are performing one of the key acts of leadership.

Why "Living Stories"?

Arie de Geus, former head of strategic planning for Shell Oil, in his study of companies that enjoy extraordinarily long lives, observed that "like all organisms, the living company exists primarily for its own survival and improvement, to fulfill its potential *and* to become as great as it can be."[21] The living story reinforces that same impulse to greatness. It is an articulation in story form of the past, present and possible future of a group or organization. It expresses identity, current reality and hopes and aspirations. The story includes the path that needs to be taken by the hero or the organization to become great. A living story also "anoints role models, imparts values, and shows how to execute indescribably complex tasks."[22]

The living story differs from other kinds of stories in that it is a work-in-progress. Part of the story has already happened, part is what is current or about to happen, and part is what wants and needs to happen. So this living story builds from a recognizable current reality to a possible future in ways that excite and motivate listeners. That journey describes worlds to which those listeners will want to belong, opening a future for them that they want to be part of.[23] Because there is tension between what is (current reality) and what could be, the living story has energy, hope and promise.

Living stories are rooted in what wants and needs to happen. They begin with good listening *before* the story gets told. The listening may be to you or to others, to the market, to customers, to your community or constituencies. This is listening for people's aspirations and purpose. It is hearing their emotions, their moods, their assessments or judgments and what they believe is possible. Through such listening, the listener is changed. The possibilities evolve and develop.

People instinctively differentiate the living story from the stagnating or dead-end stories human beings sometimes create and become lost in. Stagnating stories are full of blame, of historical reasons for how things are and of assumptions of fixed identity. Such stories are often told over and over, sometimes passionately and sometimes with resignation, in the vain hope that by doing the same things one will get different results.

If a new living story is not repeated, again and again until it is equally familiar, it will be dismissed, ignored or replaced by the current story. Telling it is what makes a story live, moves it from rumor to reality. Told often and well, the living story gets woven into the fabric of our collective and individual identities and becomes the basis for new possibilities. Think about a time you changed a behavior and no one noticed. For example, you stopped being late for appointments, but people continued to think of you as someone who was always late. Until that new story of you as an on-time person is told — and repeated many times — people won't replace the old story with the new one.

How Story Works

One superb example of the power of a story comes from Ford Motor Company in the late 1970s and early 1980s. There came a day when *everybody* at Ford — from plant floor people to the CEO — got it: "I have to change how I am behaving today or there may not be a Ford tomorrow." They came up with a new story about Ford, a story that we still know today: "Quality is Job One." Those four short words brilliantly encapsulated a whole story. Ford employees knew what the call to action was (survival), who the heroes were (anyone who fought for quality), what the monsters were (quality failures), where the journey would take them (from last to first) and how they would be the same yet different when they returned home (known for quality throughout the world).

Yet a good story alone is not enough. People have to believe the story. So the first time a worker on an assembly line decided to take management at its word and stopped the line when he saw a quality defect, there was a collective inhalation of breath throughout the company — because, prior to that, *stopping the line got you fired.*

Regardless of the reason, no one ever stopped the line. So the entire company waited and watched. When management made that worker a hero, there was a collective exhalation. People knew the story was real. People could believe it, own it and honor it. People were galvanized by that story. And that story carried Ford for nearly twenty years, coming close in the late 1990s to toppling GM from its perch as the biggest of the Big Three American automakers.[24]

Simple and Explicit, Complex and Implicit[25]

Any industry or organization will have stories, whether they are deliberately built or not. Stories are a way to embed a lot of information in a highly compact form; yet it can be dangerous to make the story itself too complex. In *Leading Minds*, Howard Gardner observes that a simpler story will always overtake a complex story.[26] This is a source of the power of Jesus' parables. With a truly great story, there is no "dumbing it down" for supposedly lesser folk; the story holds, clear and consistent no matter the audience. The hallmark of a powerful story is that competing versions don't hold up and have little credibility.

Yet, in today's media-soaked world, one often loses sight of what constitutes a real story. The great stories are both simple and explicit; at the same time, they're complex and implicit. Such stories tell you what is the call to action, who the heroes are, the nature of the journey and the monsters that will be encountered, as well as implying how things will be different when the journey is over. Such stories make "true north" apparent, and thus function as a guide to daily behavior.

It is important to distinguish between a tag line and a story. "Quality is Job One" tells a story. "Civil servants deliver America's dream," which came from a young NASA leader,[27] tells a powerful story. Again, it is clear what the call to action is, who the heroes are, what the nature of the journey is and what at least some of the monsters might be, as well as how things will be different at the end of the journey. Accenture's "Now it gets interesting," Nike's "Just

Do It," or Volkswagen's "Drivers Wanted," however, are tag lines. They do not tell a story. They don't give direction or tell those listening how to behave in complex situations.

The Language of the Great Stories

Earlier I observed that telling the story helps make it so. There is also important language characteristically embedded in a great living story, language in the form of implicit or explicit phrases or speech patterns, sometimes called "declarations."

The first of these is the declaration *No*. *No* in a living story sets boundaries and tells listeners what behavior is unacceptable. This makes it possible for characters in the story to opt out, to decline — by promising not to do something. The second is the declaration *Yes*. When the story tells participants they can say *no*, at least some of the time, that means they can say *yes* and mean it. Their *yes* is not a lie. The living story allows us to know when and how to make and keep promises to one another.

The third important declaration is *I don't know*. In a great living story, there must be space for learning, room for people to admit their ignorance and ask their questions. People are not punished for learning. In fact, they are rewarded, for these are the people who ultimately learn how to defeat their monsters. Fourth is the declaration of gratitude — ways and times to say *thank you* to one another and to the world. We know when agreements are complete (and another chapter of the story ended) because we are thanked for our contributions. We freely express appreciation for one another and our progress on the journey and move on to the next challenge.

Finally, in a living story there is forgiveness. People apologize and say *I'm sorry* when they have hurt someone or not kept a promise, unintentionally or not. They ask forgiveness as well: *Will you forgive me?* Not every living story overtly contains these five declarations, but every great story has space for all of them.[28] In fact, the presence of these conversations provides extremely valuable markers as to the health of an organization or a story.

The Structure of Stories

The listening for the living story described earlier does not produce a story in jewel-like form, each facet neatly polished. One role leaders often play is to detect the diamond-in-the-rough and help the group do the cutting and polishing. (Keep in mind, the leader is not necessarily the person in charge.) Every great living story has the same fundamental architecture to which we have been referring. The individual or the group is called to leave the known world — their past and present — to search for, track down or explore some unknown. On the journey, the heroes enter the "pit" where they must encounter monsters. (In actuality, the monsters are a projection of the fears they must confront if they are to learn, grow and develop.)

This is the pivotal point: the heroes may stay stuck in the pit, or they may engage the monster, win that battle and climb back out, transformed and wiser, ready to tell a new story of courage and triumph. This metamorphosis, this learning through confronting fear must be done to complete this part of the journey, be changed in the process and become ready for new action. Often, stories and their heroes do get stuck in the pit. The heroes are afraid to meet the monster, accept uncertainty or allow change. They may be so fearful that they do not even admit to being stuck in the pit. These are the dead-end stories discussed earlier.

Conclusion: Find a Story That's Worth Your Life

A key to effective leadership is building and transmitting a compelling story. You are abdicating your role — within your family, your organization or your industry — if you don't have a compelling story to tell. Great stories help people distinguish between what is merely important and what is fundamental. In other words, stories are how people make meaning out of their activity.

Stories are also the way we think about our lives — past, present and future. Great stories are always implicitly about an increase in maturity. Lacking a story, people have no way to explain their work and their lives, to make them make sense and have value. The quality of the story in which an individual or an organization lives is reflected in the language they use as well as the way they act. With a great story, one that is not just told but also practiced, ordinary people truly do extraordinary things. Such a story is worth investing a lifetime in.

This is just as true today as it was once upon a time.

III | LEADERSHIP'S STORY

It may be that when we no longer know what to do,
we have come to our real work
and that when we no longer know which way to go
we have begun our journey.

~ WENDELL BERRY

The current stories about leadership do not prepare us adequately for the times. A new story may not be needed: it may be that we need to circle back to a very old story that is reinvented every time the world reaches a certain level of complexity. To paraphrase Lao Tzu, the Chinese Taoist philosopher, "The bad leaders are hated and feared, the good leaders are loved and admired, and with the great leaders, the people say, 'We did it ourselves.'" He said this in sixth-century, B.C., China, another place and time of great organizational and cultural complexity.

How is it that truly mature leaders seem to accomplish so much simply through their being, their presence? It is as though, through their being, they open a space. Inside that space, as the sense-making and problem solving proceed, people seem to enlarge, to glow with the illumination of their own call, and to resonate together. The result is powerfully coordinated action. Mature leaders, people who have grown intellectually, emotionally, morally and spiritually, seem able to release magic, make the story alive and full of wonder and energy. By being themselves, they enable all the calls to merge into a story of deep commitment and profound results.

In this chapter, we will look at three overlapping stories about leaders, stories that describe what we believe is possible and necessary in a leader. The first of these is the oft-told story of the heroic leader. The second is the more current story of the collaborative leader. The third is the story of leadership when things must make sense before action can be taken — the story of dialogic leadership.

The Old Story

The earliest story is that of the leader as the solitary figure who does it all himself through physical prowess and cunning. This is the hero/leader who out of a combination of skill, generosity and vain-gloriousness, slays the monster. As Beowulf says, "Behavior that's admired is the path to power among people everywhere."[29] The legacy of the equation of leader with superhero, is a burden that we still struggle with today.

Wilfred Drath, in *The Deep Blue Sea: Rethinking the Source of Leadership*, names this "First Principle Leadership." He notes that such a leader:

> ... being the exemplar of what is right, good, powerful, intelligent, is naturally the best person to provide direction and to know what needs to be done. Knowing what needs to be done does not mean simply doing whatever it might occur to the leader to do; it means knowing what makes sense to the community, what the needs and desires of the community are, what will work in the context of the community.[30]

Drath observes that this story about leadership — heroic First Principle leadership — like all stories about leadership is one that is jointly created and held between leader and followers. He further notes that, "Dominance and charisma come from this perfect attunement between leader and follower in the shared creation of a kind of leadership that creates a leader who is irreplaceable."[31]

In that irreplaceability, of course, lies the weakness of such leadership. When such a king dies, the kingdom falls to ruin:

neither King Arthur's nor Beowulf's kingdom survived their deaths. When the leader single-handedly embodies all the virtues, is the exemplar of all that the community wants and needs, then others in the community or organization fail to develop the capacity to lead. Family-run businesses and start-ups struggle with these issues of succession. It is equally the story of Coca-Cola after Robert Goizeuta's death, and the risk that Intel and Southwest Airlines run, post-Andy Grove and Herb Kelleher. Will there be new heroes to replace the old ones?

The Current Story

As society becomes more complex, the demands on the leadership story also become more complex, transcending yet including the old story.[32] In a more complex setting, truth and leadership are no longer the purview of the one who can best articulate the community's "beckoning, collective future."[33] Instead, many people must contribute their information and insight for that future to be clear, and they work to influence one another in that process. Drath's Second Principle leadership story thus becomes focused on collaboration and influencing. The most influential person is the leader. "If commitment in the first principle can be called loyalty, commitment in the second principle is *alignment*."[34]

The use of collaboration and alignment as buzzwords in both the public and private sectors in the last twenty years reflect the influence-driven nature of large organizations. Leaders are encouraged to build alignment in their organizations, whether through Hewlett-Packard's consensus-driven *hoshin*[35] process, through sharing learning (as in "learning organizations"), through organization-wide strategic planning (such as the "reinventing government" efforts of the 1990s) or through knowledge management and dialogue.

In the Second Principle leadership story, leaders publicly seek opinions from all sides before setting a direction, and that direction is thus understood to have taken into account all those differing points of view. Such leadership is perceived as interpersonal and influential, as well as more tolerant of ambiguity.[36] This story, too, is jointly created and held between leader and followers. Yet even this collaborative approach is not adequate for the level of challenges faced in a globally linked environment filled with powerful economic, nationalistic and religious belief systems.

The Future Story

In the old stories, the slaying of one monster often simply provokes the waking of the next, as it did in Beowulf, when slaying Grendel awakened Grendel's mother. In today's world, we see this same dynamic repeated. Legislation to conquer one monster begets a new one, as it has, for example, repeatedly done in American campaign financing. Similarly, pension plans established decades ago to keep employees secure now threaten to destroy the companies such as General Motors and USX that must pay them. So, too, must our old and current leadership stories recognize they have generated a new monster — that of a world grown in many places too complex for the First and Second Principles' stories of dominance and influence.

We now stand on the cusp of a third story about leadership. It is the story that needs to happen when we operate in a world too complex to simply continue making decisions and solving problems. *It is a world where we no longer know what the problems actually are or what decisions to make.* We have to make sense of our world before we can solve problems and make decisions. As Drath observes, we then need:

> ... to learn a language ... that allows people to know what they agree and disagree about and why, to know what is and is not a problem, what does and does not need deciding. It is a search for shared understanding (which is not the same as agreement) on which the hard work of problem solving and decision making can be built.[37]

This is dialogic leadership, where leaders can admit "I don't have all the answers," and invite others to help them figure it out together.

Returning to the Power of the Story

A story is required as a way of making meaning out of the data flood. Stories, told and retold, framed from one point of view and then another, become the vehicle for sense-making.[38] Shared stories let us see, hear and feel one another's experiences. Cutting and pasting new stories together allows us to taste and smell new possibilities. Weaving disparate strands together lets us intuitively sense what is and isn't working, what might or might not work in the future.

Stories invite everyone into a new and different kind of conversation, a conversation for meaning-making and possibility. Stories prevent analysis paralysis. At the same time, stories can prevent premature action. Because they operate in our emotional, rather than our analytic brains, stories protect us from the power of the nay-sayers and critics, who always have reasons something won't work and never make suggestions about how something *can* work. Through stories, a path can indeed be found without rigid dogma or deadening piles of information that don't even bring knowledge, let alone wisdom.

In the early 1990s, MIT's Dialogue Project began working with health-care providers in Grand Junction, Colorado. In a community in which the providers were in bitter competition with one another, a safe haven was created for the three CEOs of competing hospitals to explore their old stories and create new ones. Each one entered the dialogue process convinced through their research that the only path to success was to "beat" the other two. Findings published in the Project's Annual Report stated that:

> As they explored the roots of one conflict after another, they realized the inadequacies of their well-worn stories concerning the status quo. Each began to realize that his or

her interpretation of others' behavior was insufficient grounds for judgment.[39]

Through their conversations together, they began to build a new story about health care in their community. As a result, they were able to come to an amicable and collaborative distribution of the community's medical resources that resulted in higher quality care for the citizens of Grand Junction in a surprisingly short time.[40]

A Different Path to Leadership Development

It is often argued that love (as I defined it earlier), dialogue, clarity and compassion 1) are not actually valid leadership tools, and 2) have no place in business. Further, it is said, we lack the tools with which to engage whole organizations in meaning-making, let alone problem-solving. Yet these arguments long ago lost their validity.

There are now decades of solid research confirming the positive bottom-line impact of behavioral manifestations of love, such as service, integrity, trust and respect. *Fortune Magazine's* annual "100 Best Places to Work" issue consistently reports that companies where people feel valued and respected make healthy profits. A study in the early 1990s showed a 756 percent increase in net profits over eleven years in companies which valued multiple internal and external stakeholder satisfaction and involvement.[41] In *Working with Emotional Intelligence*, Daniel Goleman cites literally hundreds more studies with similar results.

Why is the research ignored? Why are our institutions, our businesses, our governments in the shape they are? Why are our communities in the shape they are? Why are our schools in disrepair? Why is the idea of public office anathema to so many bright, educated, ambitious people? If they know what needs to be done, why are our leaders not doing it?

The answer is deceptively simple: *They are not really leaders.* First, whether in the public or private sector, we do not promote leaders;

we promote managers. Managers do things that can be measured; leaders change the agenda. Managers seem safer. Second, we have made the role of leader untenable: we demand that leaders lead everywhere, not just in their own domain. We do not like our leaders as flawed human beings.

Because they are fundamentally managers, many of our leaders simply do as they are told. And what they are told is primarily "Make money, fast" and "Don't rock the boat politically." So the people we call "leaders" sacrifice ethics and long-term thinking on the altar of generating 20 percent per year increased return on investment (ROI), or they govern via polls, addressing themselves only to what the majority think they want this week. *And yes, it is just that simple.*

And it is just that complex. Because there is only one way this can change; we must *all* begin to address the hard issues of growing up. That means stepping up to our own individual leadership responsibilities. Whether we are twenty or forty or sixty, we must acknowledge the captaincy of our own lives — that no one else decides for us how our lives will be. We must each accept that there will be times to lead in our lives and times to follow, times to know when to simply accept our call and lead from it and times to give wise counsel to those who are leading.

That duality of leading and following is fundamental to a deeply missing component of civic, social and business life today — the role of the elder. Whether it be on a company's Board of Directors, a non-profit's Board of Advisors, or any of a number of other roles, we need mature people who know when to lead and when to follow, people who have reached elderhood. (Elderhood and leadership are not meant to be synonymous here. Nor is elderhood a function of age, though age plays a role for many of us.)

In *Community and Growth*, Jean Vanier comments wisely on the relationship between leaders and elders:

Many leaders are fearful of and too dependent on their community council. They do not seem to be able to give true leadership. I am not sure that a community council can be prophetic, and frequently leadership needs to be prophetic. A council made up of elders is important; it permits the leaders to see all sides of a question. But a council will tend to be conservative: "We have always done things this way." Elders can block the growth and evolution of change. A leader needs to know how to use the council wisely, how to help it and how to be helped by it to come to the right decisions.[42]

Maturity — intellectual, emotional, moral and spiritual — is what gives both the current leader and the elders room to engage in meaning-making conversations that lead to the kinds of decisions that grow healthy communities and healthy workplaces. Maturity enables an organization to hold the tension of disagreements, to honor the reality of multiple needs in complex settings and to discern new possibilities without succumbing to anxiety or arbitrary solutions. A leadership rooted in love generates such maturity.

Moreover, we need always to be able to draw some portion of our leadership from our elders. All three of Drath's stories about leadership — heroic, collaborative or dialogic — may be applicable at any given moment. Some people come naturally to one or another of those principles, finding one particular path easy and comfortable. Their story's path may be one in which, having reached the limits of their capability, they step aside to allow someone else to take the organization or community to the next level. Clearly, this takes great self-awareness and maturity.

The closest analogy today to this kind of mature leadership role is perhaps an unlikely one: that of the community organizer. As Ernesto J. Cortes Jr., a member of the national staff of the Industrial Areas Foundation (IAF), a source of much of the organizing tradition in the United States since the 1930s, notes:

The job of an organizer is to agitate. Now, people have the stereotype of what agitation is. But in the sense the IAF teaches it, the agitator raises questions, gets people to look at their choices, to look at their options, to understand that power depends upon consent. The ethics of power really hovers around the question of how you go about obtaining consent. You can obtain consent by force or violence. You can obtain consent by deceit, by lying to people. You can obtain consent by manipulating people, withholding information, rendering them incompetent. But finally you can learn to obtain consent through informed judgment.[43]

In today's world, we have many leaders whose leadership is based on obtaining consent through force or deceit or withholding. They are not the leaders we need. The type of training that community organizing provides might be the best training we could offer in our leadership programs today, certainly far more useful than the MBA and executive development programs that currently pass as leadership training.

If, as Joe Jaworski, founder of the American Leadership Forum says, "Leadership is all about the release of human possibilities,"[44] then teaching leaders how to "obtain consent through informed judgment" means that we release the power of leadership that enrolls, leadership that invites the world to participate in the making of meaning and the taking of action without scapegoating or blaming. That is the leadership we truly need.

Self-Authorizing Leadership[45]

Third Principle leadership, this sense-making and story-building form of leadership, gives leaders room for a new kind of voice. As Lewis Hyde describes it in his introduction to Thoreau's essays, this is a prophetic voice, in the sense that "the prophet speaks of things that will be true in the future:"[46]

... under the spell of the prophetic voice, we can, sometimes, sort the true from the false and begin to move. We find ourselves in a story that makes sense, and such stories engender action.[47]

Prophetic voices invite us all into leadership, each to add a piece to the story. What we add is driven by the nature of our call: "The prophetic voice doesn't just uncover the world; it uncovers the eyes."[48] In that uncovering, we see clearly what we mean to do. We no longer wait for others to provide leadership; we understand we are authorized to provide it for ourselves. "We are ushered into an adult-adult conversation with our own powers."[49] This brings about more leadership, rather than less, more accountability rather than less. Such prophetic leadership also invites us into a bigger story, onto a larger playing field.

With self-authorizing leadership, there is, paradoxically, more and less of us. As David Whyte notes,

> One of the outer qualities of great captains, great leaders, great bosses is that they are unutterably themselves ... The best stay true to a conversation that is the sum of their own strange natures and the world they inhabit, and do not attempt to mimic others in order to get on.[50]

Strangely, these leaders do not achieve their identity at our expense. In this way of being absolutely who they are, such leaders also give us room to be absolutely who we are. And when we can be who we are, egos tend to dissipate. Open to our largest calling, we no longer need the ego-driven paraphernalia of our analytic self, the part of us that weighs, measures and constantly compares.[51] We don't worry about "they got more than I did and it's not fair." We focus instead on the larger demands, a compelling vision of what wants and needs to happen in the world. As Noury Al-Khaledy, an Intel manager commented,

The key to having an apolitical environment is that you have a burning vision of success for the organization and the ability to subordinate yourself to that vision. That vision is more important than your other personal goals. If you can't do that, then no one who's following you can be asked to or will do it.[52]

This subordination to the larger goal reflects a profound developmental step. We move into service and belonging. This is elderhood. As such, it is not a function of years, but of maturity.

One example of a leader with a prophetic voice is Eleanor Josaitis, who runs a remarkable program called Focus:Hope that combines for-profit and non-profit activities on a forty-acre campus in downtown Detroit. Those activities include a training program for machinists, 51,000 volunteers, several manufacturing companies, a food program that feeds 48,000 people and a day-care center. "We're in the business of giving people opportunities. It's up to them to accept each opportunity, take it and run with it," says Josaitis. Focus:Hope prides itself on developing "renaissance engineers," people who not only understand technology but are strong communicators and understand marketing, sales and finance.[53] This is definitely a bigger story than the usual non-profit organization.

Another, and perhaps the most striking current example of such prophetic leadership, was the establishment of South Africa's Truth and Reconciliation Commission. While Archbishop Desmond Tutu is the public figure most well-known, the Commission required enormous leadership from leaders throughout the country. Encouraging truth-telling by offering amnesty for admission of acts of violence committed between 1960 and 1994 represented a remarkable effort on the part of South Africa and its people to come to terms with an excruciating history. Recognizing that people's stories needed to be told if healing was ever going to occur represented an extraordinary level of leadership maturity.

Coming Full Circle: Leadership's Paradoxes

How does this process work? What are such leaders actually doing? Deep in our neurology, in the brain structure of every human being, lies our limbic system, also known as the mammalian brain, because we share this structure with all mammals. An older part of our brains than the analytical and synthesizing neo-cortex, the limbic system is tied to emotions and the heart. As psychiatrists Thomas Lewis, Fari Amini and Richard Lannon note in *A General Theory of Love,* "Who we are and who we become depends, in part, on whom we love."[54] By love, they too mean that capacity to care deeply about others and seek their best interests. It would appear that, through their integrity and trust-worthiness, such leaders activate this emotional part of our neurology, the part that actually allows us to change.

Lewis, Amini and Lannon conclude that deep caring carves new neurological pathways, literally redesigning the way our mammalian or emotional brains work. These actual neurological revisions or changes made possible by love are central to effective individual and collective leadership. They generate the increased capacity for emotional, intellectual, moral and spiritual development that underlies almost every form of leadership development.

Jim Collins concludes his chapter on leadership in *Good to Great* by discussing the question of whether one has to sacrifice having a great life in order to work for a great company. Just the opposite, he concludes: the leaders of great companies "clearly loved what they did, largely because they loved who they did it with. For no matter what we achieve, if we don't spend the vast majority of our time with people we love and respect, we cannot possibly have a great life."[55] Even when working for a great cause, one must ultimately be able to love and respect those with whom one works to sustain the effort. Love, as defined earlier, in leadership becomes both cause and effect, both source and action.

The French priest, Jean Vanier, whom I quoted earlier on elderhood, founded the first l'Arche, a remarkable community for the mentally handicapped and their helpers which has been replicated in Europe, Africa and Australia. As he watched community after community grow, he observed:

> As people grow in love, as their hearts become more open, and as a community in its narrow sense becomes mature, so does the reality of the community, of "my people," get larger.[56]

Shanksville, Pennsylvania, was the site of the crash of United Airlines flight 93 on September 11, 2001. Since then, the town has found itself uniquely called to stewardship as caretakers of grief, working hard to honor the heroism as well as the loss that Flight 93 represents. Opening their hearts to the families who lost a relative in the crash, as well as the thousands who have come to visit the crash site, has expanded their sense of community and responsibility. This enlarged sense of community is precisely the underpinning of leadership's recognition of its role as steward, in service to a greater good. From the county coroner who arranged a memorial service for all the bereaved families to the second grade teacher whose idea gathered the entire township into the school parking lot to spell out "Thank You" for the messages and gifts that had flooded the town from across the U.S. in an aerial photograph, leadership emerged.[57] With such enlarging, people grow also in clarity and compassion.

Conclusion: Being the New Story

Mature leaders are people who, amongst other abilities, can activate all three leadership principles (heroic, collaborative and dialogic — the three leadership stories described by Drath) and who can include the full range of behaviors in their repertoire. Part of maturity is being fully responsible for saying what needs to be said (speaking the truth) or doing what needs to be done (pointing to hope) without grandiosity, without the secret belief that you are responsible for *everything*. You understand that there are others to help. You speak of stewardship, of gratitude, of forgiveness and of love. You can act in these ways as well, creating the space in which others can operate at their finest. These are the grown-up themes of the great stories.

Comfortable with facing reality and confident that once the sense-making is complete, all things can be (collectively) handled, the mature leader becomes almost transparent, a kind of ego-less force in whose presence all blossom.

These are people who tell the future by being that future. In so doing, they make possible a new story for all of us. They speak the truth of the heart and, by so speaking, point to hope. This is the new story that our understanding of leadership needs. When we understand this story, we all can become a part of it.

LEADERSHIP IS A CHOICE
BARBARA WAUGH OF HEWLETT-PACKARD'S E-INCLUSION

Barbara Waugh is the author of **The Soul in the Computer: The Story of a Corporate Revolutionary.** *A long-time radical activist, she joined Hewlett-Packard (HP) twenty years ago and used her successive positions as company recruiting manager, personnel director and worldwide change manager for the renowned HP Labs to transform HP's corporate culture. Along the way she invented and discovered a set of "radical tools" for introducing practical change and energizing altruism at all levels of the organization. She is the co-founder of e-inclusion, a new HP business dedicated to bringing the benefits of the Internet economy to the poor around the world.*

Barb doesn't leave her values at home. She has a doctorate in psychology and organizational behavior, a master's degree in theology and comparative literature and has served on the Board of Directors for the State of the World Forum, the Board of Directors for the Pacific Cultural Conservancy International and the Board of Advisers for the Global Fund for Women. She lives in Northern California with her partner and their two children.

I put this conversation first because Barb so clearly challenges the notions of heroic and even collaborative leadership. Her own book gives example after example of innovative ways to engage people in meaning-making conversations — the Third Principle leadership story. I also found her understanding of story to be profoundly enriching.

LISA MARSHALL: Barbara, you and I share a common conviction about the power of story to help move and motivate people. I want

| 35 |

to explore how you have experienced a "call" to leadership in yourself and others, the roles others play in your leadership, what your leadership journey has been like, what issues you have faced, the ways in which you have changed and the ways in which you have stayed the same. First, what's your definition of leadership?

BARBARA WAUGH: A leader is anyone who has a very big and compelling story of how it could all turn out, who then identifies and amplifies positive deviance within whatever system they're attempting to move, using the system's strengths to migrate it to where it needs to be. For example, the story I hold is that the corporate sector must join the non-profit and public sectors to step up to our share of stewardship for the planet. Studies on the diffusion of innovation have demonstrated that you need only three percent of a system to be firmly convinced of a new direction, to transform the system. Three percent of a given company, three percent of the corporate sector — these are doable in my lifetime.

LM: What is its source?

BW: The source is different for different people. The drive to lead is the leader's passion for how they want the world to be, which she or he may not be conscious of (and doesn't have to be). For me, it's pragmatic; I have a better life, more interesting, fewer depressions, greater joy when I live as one of these passionate people than when I don't, and I know I have that choice. There's massive evidence to justify cynicism, but it just doesn't get you a good life. Why not live inside a story that gives you a good life and has the potential for turning out the way you would like?

The sources of leadership have been greatly mystified. I say to people, "Do you want a good life or not? Do you want to be happy or sad? Have fun or be miserable? It's not at the mercy of the evidence; the evidence is too complex to reliably predict a future from, so take note of it, and then go on and choose the way you want it to be."

LM: What was your first experience, or discovery, of your ability to lead?

BW: I sometimes have had the experience of people coming up to me from earlier parts of my life saying, "Do you remember when you...?" And I think they have the wrong person. So there may be something that was happening for other people through working with me that wasn't yet happening for me.

For me, my first experience of community organizing is a more useful reference point. Or when I started the first feminist newspaper column in Madison, Wisconsin. There was an amazing, unprecedented response: I was announced at parties, my life was threatened several times. I didn't care for it, but I did notice it. I was startled by the power in that role of creating reality. It was pretty chilling to understand the implicit responsibility, that what you attended to or ignored, choice-fully or inadvertently, had consequences. There was tremendous responsibility there.

LM: How has your gift changed over time?

BW: I truly don't think leadership is a gift. Calling it a gift is part of the voodoo of leadership. Leadership is accessible to anyone who wants it. It's a choice; you decide what you want your life to be about and you go after it. It's not that mystical. The three percent I was talking about earlier, those who make the choice to take responsibility for their lives, live inside a big story. And others flock to them — most people want to be in a big story.

Today I'm more mindful of both the power and the responsibility, and less startled, not as thrown by what comes out of it. I no longer hold any specific idea of how things will turn out. My Rock of Gibraltar is the big story, but the subplots can't be predicted. Now I watch for valences, directions, projects and people that align or could be "framed" to align with the big story, and I help things turn out that way.

LM: When do you know you've received the call to leadership?

BW: As I said, I'm not so sure leaders are "called." When I see it in others, it's because they're answering a question that people are living with but haven't, many times, even yet asked; giving words to the unarticulated longings. Probably true for me as well.

LM: How do you know the call has been answered?

BW: I know it is answered when I feel I'm contributing, when people light up around me. I like the idea of being a messenger. I feel I've answered the call when I've transmitted the message without messing it up too much.

LM: What do you as a leader need from others in order to be effective? What roles do you need them to play?

BW: I work in one domain across all functions — the generative, the part that makes new things happen. I'm all over the company; there's no job description for it. I'm very lucky that that didn't mean to my management that I therefore couldn't do the job. Since all the operational systems require you to have some label or other in the book of jobs, we went with "Research Engineer" which isn't as far off as some of the job descriptions I've had. One way to look at what I'm doing is that I'm developing and refining change management tools for complex systems.

I also need to be coupled with someone who's as passionate about making ideas operational as I am about visioning. It's unfortunate — tragic, in fact — that I get the credit and they do the work. As long as our recognition and reward systems are so skewed in favor of the vocal visionary over the quiet implementer, in favor of the one over the many that it actually takes to get things done, we'll continue to be blind to the potential brilliance in the company.

The ongoing lament in companies that we haven't got the right people or the best people — well, I don't buy it. What I see is that we haven't gotten the right and the best of the people we have. If we did, we'd realize we have the perfect people for what we need to do and where we need to go.

LM: Describe your own leadership journey.

BW: Like most people, I always thought great leaders were born, not made, were gifted and special in ways that would never be mine. I figured the best I could ever do was find one and follow. What I didn't realize was that what makes a leader is a great story and that if you pick a big story and live inside it, great people will be attracted to you and you'll be lifted up by them.

I also thought that life was about spending a few minutes or less figuring out what you wanted and then spending the rest of your life going after it. Our whole culture tells us it's like that. Think of the structure of movies, advertisements, the myths of western culture — think of Jason and the Golden Fleece, the search for the Holy Grail, *Star Wars*, etc. How, in fact, it works in my life is that most of my life is figuring out what I want. When that's really clear, all kinds of things fall into place and I get what I want very quickly.

The real quest is for the story: *What story is worth your life?* Take your time with that, go on a search. If your search leaves you with less than a story worth your life, then invent one. Search for or invent the story; put together the pieces from other stories that compel you. Once you have the story, everything gets attracted to it, the pieces fall in place and things work out.

LM: What gets in the way of your leadership?

BW: Schedules that don't align with my own rhythms get in the way. I contribute more when I stay out of the system. The kinds of intelligence and insights required to shift the system are best fostered outside the system. My best "shape shifting" happens in the hot tub, on a long bike ride or taking a nap. You think differently lying down than sitting up — it's literally a different point of view.

LM: What are the dilemmas that cause you the greatest concern?

BW: My biggest dilemmas are when I start getting into control, having to make it turn out a certain way, worrying about "what if?" If I can live in the big story that doesn't happen, but I still get catapulted into the daily drama and lose that bigger picture. And I'm still trying to understand the role of informal leaders in making large system change happen.

LM: What do you understand about leadership now that you didn't five or ten years ago?

BW: I understand that what I mean by leadership is authenticity, and that it's a choice. It's not bestowed, it's not a gift, and it's something you can choose and if you do, you're in for a ride; it's worth your life! By authenticity, I mean both being true to your self and inventing a self that's worth being true to.

CALL TO ACTION

IV THE GIFT OF TRUE LONGING
THE CALL TO ACTION

> *Some are born great,*
> *some achieve greatness,*
> *and some have greatness thrust upon 'em.*
>
> ~ SHAKESPEARE, *Twelfth Night* (MALVOLIO)

What enables one person to see new possibilities in a situation where others see only bleakness? What is that impulse to forward motion, that deep internal drive to tell a bigger story, make a difference, seek greatness, create beauty or order or see a new world into being? What makes one person willing to stand up and say, "I will take responsibility for making X happen" when others don't move? What "calls" one of us now, another not until much later and some of us never?

In Campbell's story architecture, the call represents the starting point of every great story. The call is an ancient idea, one that exists in many spiritual and cultural traditions. It refers to the moment of awakening in which you recognize that you are being summoned to a particular path or role. In the hero's journey, the call is the wake-up moment, when the hero begins to see what she or he must do next and begins to feel inexorably drawn to the journey.

Hearing the Call

The call can be a quiet moment of realization or a trumpet call to action. Moses got his call as a burning bush and Joan of Arc as voices in her father's garden; most of us do not receive the call quite so vividly. Indeed, the call's form is multiple and varied; it can be as literal as a phone call asking one to take on a new role at church or work, or as subtle as a recurring thought that "this situation really doesn't need to be this way." It can come as a request for help, a sense of desperation or as a challenge — "You think you could do

43

better?" The call can come as the nagging realization that no one else is going to do anything, and it can come as an internal impulse so profound you do not recognize it until after you have responded because you are too busy *doing*.

Campbell notes that calls are regularly resisted. Years ago, Bill Cosby did a wonderful routine about God calling Noah to build the Ark. Noah's first response is to ignore Him several times. Eventually, Noah says "What? Whaddyawant?" in an annoyed voice. After listening to the command, he responds sarcastically, "Right ... what's an Ark?" and finally, "Why me?" At that, God answers with a loud crack of thunder. Variations on all these responses are frequently recorded in myth and legend, and reported in our workplaces today.

Accepting the Call

Accepting the call is the starting point for every great story. In choosing (consciously or otherwise) to accept it or not, there are powerful possibilities for self-betrayal and self-fulfillment at play. Do we own our choices or hold others responsible for them? "Well, I would have responded, but this person or that situation wouldn't let me." Or, "It's not my fault, it wasn't clear that was a call to *me*." True heroes may not be happy about it, but they accept the call. In Peter Jackson's film version of *The Fellowship of the Ring*, Frodo says, "I wish the ring had never come to me. I wish none of this had happened," to which Gandalf replies, "So do all who live to see such times, but that is not for them to decide. All we have to decide is what to do with the time that is given to us."[58]

In the old stories, ignoring a call often resulted in a louder, harsher one, until the designee accepted his role. In our noisy, complex world, some may feel it's just as hard to know which calls to not accept as it is to recognize a call at all. The reality is that a true call *cannot* be ignored. The more authoritative, visible and unmistakable a call is, the more transformative it will be.

Calls have two key aspects, exquisitely summarized in David Whyte's phrase "the gift of true longing."[59] One is the "gift," both in the sense of ability and in the sense of being given a call, and the other is "true longing" — the deep yearning in us that responds to the call when we (finally) recognize it.

True Longing

In true longing lie the headwaters of the leadership imperative, that profound internal impulse to somehow make a difference, where all leadership starts. A call cannot and will not be heard without true longing. Whyte describes "feeling the currents of the great desire, carrying time towards tomorrow."[60] Like a tiny spring high in the mountains that ultimately becomes a fast flowing river, the great desire, for many, is latent. It remains hidden in a deep place until life calls it out, as it did with David Kaczynski, brother of convicted Unabomber Ted Kaczynski. He found himself playing a major role in national dialogues around victims' rights, retribution, healing, revenge, forgiveness and ending the death penalty, as he came to grips with having turned his brother in. As he sought reconciliation with and forgiveness by his brother's victims, he found himself taking a public role he never anticipated or asked for. "It seems like one thing has led to another and that I want to bring some greater good out of something that was unimaginably bad."[61]

True longing is what makes us strong enough to overcome fear, shyness, doubt and insecurity, both on the part of the person taking a leadership role and those around her. In a *Harvard Business Review* article drawn from his book *Good to Great*, author and researcher Jim Collins describes transformative leaders as possessing a "paradoxical mixture of personal humility and professional will ... timid and ferocious, shy and fearless."[62] As an example:

> Asked how he turned Ford around, [Don Petersen] emphatically attributes the success to others. Says Petersen: "I want you to remember one thing. The credit here goes to

our team, not me." So low is his profile that even after he became chairman in 1985, the company proxy statement misspelled his name.[63]

When leaders find a story that they can believe in and commit to, they can focus their "true longing" and become one with the story, living it, breathing it and *being* it.

True longing seems to live at the borders of our awareness, sometimes recognized, sometimes not. "The very essence of leadership, going out ahead to show the way, derives from more than usual openness to inspiration," observed Robert Greenleaf in his seminal book, *Servant Leadership*.[64] Somewhere in the interplay between exquisite sensitivity to what wants to happen in the world and our own deepest yearnings lies a place where "your deep gladness and the world's great hunger meet."[65] In that mix of desire, will, imagination, pattern recognition, accountability and an ability to see a path to a better way or a better world, the catalytic desire that pulls us forward is formed. This desire, this pull, is "our wordless, fiery, unspoken, hardly remembered, gift of true longing."[66] And true longing *is* a gift because it generates the receptive field in which the call will finally be heard and answered.

The Gift

In his provocative work *The Gift*, Lewis Hyde reminds us that gifts can be material objects or experiences we receive. They can also be abilities we find within ourselves. The two (objects/experiences or abilities) are fundamentally the same: they come to us without our having "earned" them. So it is with the "gift" of leadership — it is a gift we both receive and give.

At its best, the gift of leadership has two elements; clarity and compassion. Clarity, seeing both the truth of what is and what could be, is central to the gift received, the gift of leadership ability. Compassion is the gift of love from leaders to others. (Though obviously, leaders also give clarity and followers, compassion.)

What is the source of both? What is the root of the leadership imperative? Contrary to popular myth, it is not our brilliant minds. It is our brilliant hearts. In *Working with Emotional Intelligence*, Daniel Goleman notes:

> *Motive* and *emotion* share the same Latin root, *motere*, "to move." Emotions are, literally, what move us to pursue our goals; they fuel our motivations, and our motives in turn drive our perceptions and shape our actions. Great work starts with great feeling.[67]

So does a great story. And so, ultimately, does great leadership.

We return here to the mammalian brain or limbic system, described in the last chapter — the part of us that is inextricably woven between head and heart, the source of the emotions that move us. Here lies the root source, the wellhead of leadership; our ability to connect with one another through clarity and/or compassion. Because leadership starts here, within the gift of connection, it is one of the hardest of essences to quantify, to pinpoint, to locate and describe with any precision. Hence, we so often revert to almost mystical language when discussing leaders and leadership.

According to Goleman, the significance of this neurological basis of leadership in the limbic system, our emotional brain center, can hardly be overstated:

> Emotional competence makes up about two thirds of the ingredients of star performance in general, but for outstanding *leaders* emotional competencies — as opposed to technical or cognitive cues — make up 80 to 100 percent of those listed by companies themselves as crucial for success.[68]

When we think our leadership ability lies in our thinking brain, the neo-cortex, we fail to recognize the root source. In assessing the best in leaders, we inevitably bow to the ineffable qualities of the heart, knowing that they are supported but not driven by the analytic work of the "head." Buried deep within our limbic system is the place where the volatile mix of motive and emotion is sorted through. When that happens, the call can be heard and the story begun.

Clarity: Discerning or Perceiving Truth Easily

Clarity, the gift received or bestowed upon the leader, is the part of the call that leaders often experience so deeply they cannot actually speak of it. Clarity enables the leader's role in building and holding the story. In doing so, it creates the container, the framework in which work can get done. Whether it is clarity about a specific goal or the new story that the situation requires, clarity about a path to collaborative problem solving, or the recognition that meaning-making must precede decision-making, leaders provide the clarity.

Leaders, when asked about this gift, usually have few words to describe what it is they do or how they do it. In fact, the question itself is often confusing, because their perceiving or discernment is so internal that they experience it as inherent in the situation and therefore obvious to everyone. In "The Sea," David Whyte refers to "tomorrow seen today, for itself."[69] That captures nicely the gift of being able to sense a future in such a way that it is real and compelling. John Greenleaf notes: "Foresight is the 'lead' that leaders have."[70] It is precisely their sense of clarity and direction that draws others to them.

Such intuitive processes require interplay (most often at an unconscious level) between what the thinking brain observes and assesses and what the mammalian brain, home to emotional memory, remembers. Pattern discernment and recognition are central to such clarity. How is this situation like others? What are the differences? What do they tell us about possibilities and how to proceed? The result of an intense awareness or sensitivity to thousands of both internal and external cues (a sense of knowing "what wants to happen"), clarity is also aided by a clear sense of what is important, what truly matters. Through such deep and often rapid neurological play, in concert with an exquisite understanding of the current reality, leaders draw upon a much wider field for hearing the call and imagining the future.

Compassion: Sharing the Suffering of Another

Compassion, the gift of sharing another's feelings and sufferings, is the gift that leaders give their followers. At its best, it is a tough and deep kindness, accepting the truth of people, recognizing who they are in their wholeness and involving them accordingly, yet not hesitating to hold them accountable to high standards of performance. Unlike niceness, which avoids confrontation and often results in increasing people's disablement and dependency, kindness or compassion enables increasing independence and interdependence. Compassion enables people to grow and stretch, taking them to places they would not have gone on their own.

The biological roots of compassion lie in our mammalian brain or limbic system's need for resonance. In *A General Theory of Love*, limbic resonance is defined as "a symphony of mutual exchange and internal adaptation where two mammals become attuned to each other's inner states."[71] Through limbic resonance — that attunement to others — the authors say that our hearts are literally strengthened, our identities clarified, our moods improved and our psychological strength increased. We have the resilience and robustness to face the unknown, to bounce back from adversity and to continue seeing possibilities.

Compassion itself is the gift of creating or amplifying limbic resonance, that experience of deep connection. With the gift of compassion, the leader extends the call to others. As Greenleaf puts it, "People grow taller when those who lead them empathize and when they are accepted for what they are."[72] Loving empathy and acceptance actually enable the leader to hold others to the highest of standards, so they feel the space and support to grow into those standards. When the mature leader responds to the call, it resonates and becomes multiplied as others, experiencing the love and trust that truth brings, freely choose to join in the response.

When Mary Cadigan, Vice President for Finance and Portfolio Technology at Fannie Mae, asked that her employees help move the computer center to a new location, she knew she was asking a lot — do your regular job all week and then work thirteen consecutive weekends with all-nighters — for no extra pay. It was a project with literally a million separate tasks. But she made it clear she knew she was asking a lot, and she was there with them, walking the floors in the middle of the night, thanking people for their efforts. She fed them dinners, midnight snacks and breakfasts, teased them, encouraged them and ultimately got them all bonuses. At the end, she threw a picnic for their families and gave tours so children could see where their parents had been. It was a "grunt work" job that made everyone feel more committed, capable and competent because of Cadigan's compassionate leadership.[73] And became a powerful story for what is possible at Fannie Mae.

Whether or not a leader is viewed as charismatic, one cannot truly lead without the ability to acknowledge and connect to others' deepest feelings and longings. In doing so, one invites others into a shared story. Amini, Lannon and Lewis observe:

> Because limbic states can leap between minds, feelings are contagious, while notions are not … That's why a movie viewed in a theater of thrilled fans is electrifying, when its living room version disappoints — it's not the size of the screen or the speakers (as the literal minded home electronics industry would have it) — it's the *crowd* that releases storytelling magic, the essential, communal, multiplied wonder.[74]

Our true longing, our craving for something bigger, something greater than ourselves, may be simply wanting to play in (or conduct) that limbic symphony. We yearn for a world to which others will also want to belong, because *then they will join us.* It is the ability to create that "essential, communal, multiplied wonder," and in doing so, generously allow each person to play a potential part in a great story, that is at the heart of the great storytelling essential to great leadership. It was precisely Cadigan's ability to create that kind of communal story that led her CEO, Franklin Raines, to say, "You performed open-heart surgery on the company for 13 weeks in a row, and we didn't even know we were operated on."[75]

Conclusion: Community is the Call

The call speaks to the essential nature of our impulse to lead. No one leads alone. With its twin gifts of clarity and compassion, the gifts of true longing, the call can never exist in a vacuum. Indeed, without the context of community, the gifts are meaningless, as, indeed, is the whole concept of leadership. We are biologically programmed to need the deep limbic resonance of being part of something greater than ourselves. When the leader's compassion extends beyond his or her own "side," beyond the tribe or the organization, then he or she is creating the type of bigger story so needed today.

Clarity about the "beckoning, collective future" of the community and compassion for its members are required for all of us as leaders. In experiencing the call and responding, both out of our own internal imperative and our gifts, we can step into the leadership role, and in doing so, find both ourselves and our community transformed.

The story begins.

THE HOW OF LEADERSHIP
RICHARD STROZZI-HECKLER OF THE
STROZZI INSTITUTE

Richard Strozzi-Heckler, PhD, is an internationally known authority on Leadership and Mastery. His wisdom about leadership has been inspired by his thirty years in business process, linguistics, psychology, biology, martial arts and philosophy. He is known for pioneering the field of somatics — the pragmatic application of skillful action, emotional balance, and spiritual vision — in such diverse arenas as business, technology, military, education, health and politics. His unique approach incorporates physical practices with conceptual learning, so that the competencies being developed actually become embodied rather than remaining good ideas forgotten in the heat of conflict. He received his doctorate in psychology from Saybrook Institute and was an NDFL Fellow at the University of Washington in 1970. He holds a sixth-degree black belt in Aikido as well as ranks in judo, jujitsu, and capoeira.

*Dr. Strozzi-Heckler is the author of the nationally acclaimed **In Search of the Warrior Spirit** (chronicling his training of the Green Berets and his vision of reclaiming traditional warrior virtues in a technologically oriented society); **The Anatomy of Change** (an embodied approach to learning and creating transformational change in performance); **Holding the Center: The Mind/Body Interface; Aikido and the New Warrior; Being Human at Work** and many other publications.*

Richard has a presence you feel the moment he walks into a room. I put his leadership conversation here because his thinking about and sensitivity to the notion of the call seemed quite striking. And while

| 53 |

he does not focus on embodying leadership per se in this interview, he clearly is someone who has thought long and hard about embodying his values, living a life congruent with and taking full responsibility for those values. It shows up quite powerfully in his work and in his way of being.

LISA MARSHALL: Richard, I know you have thought deeply about the nature of leadership and people's power to lead. Let's start there. First, how do you define leadership and what is the internal drive to lead?

RICHARD STROZZI-HECKLER: Leaders open the future for others. They organize and focus the talents and skill of others towards an observable result. They do this by producing narratives and practices in which one can design and build the future. The drive is to contribute. There is a thrust to be of value to others, to be of value, to move towards the higher ground.

LM: What is the source of that thrust?

RSH: The source is a compelling, irresistible urge toward possibility. In part, I think it's in people's genetic makeup. That's the nature part. The nurture part is growing up in an environment where there is an ethic or moral value of contribution. Or for some people, if they grow up in an environment where they're not encouraged, where they experience trauma and/or abuse, then they may use that experience to "show you," to overcome. In any case it is an urge that one follows to explore and open possibilities.

The skill or art of accessing the source of this urge is in paying attention to the stories, images, and feelings that move you, so that you then base your actions on these internal things. The quality of that attention is what moves people; energy follows attention. At the same time it is not a self-centered, obsessive compulsion. It always involves people and what they need and what you see you can offer them.

LM: What was your first experience of, or discovery of your ability to lead?

RSH: When I was young I always seemed to have a knack for organizing the other kids. I didn't feel like the boss or the best, but I could see certain things that allowed others to trust me and seek my counsel.

I began training in the martial arts as a Navy brat looking for a way to handle the harassment that inevitably went with being a new kid on a base. Ultimately I found Aikido and recognized that it called me, it was the right form for me. Then, when I had been in the discipline for a period of time, people began to look to me for decisions and direction. They also saw that I would listen to them and hear their concerns without interrupting them with my agenda. That happened in my role as an athlete and as a martial artist.

Then, in the Marine Corps, I was put in leadership roles. Other men, younger than me, started responding to something else in me. After that, I had teachers who revealed to me that there was this potential for me, and put me in front of groups. They were men and I was a young man and that was important to me. I remember in the dojo one day, when the teacher didn't show up, I was chosen to teach. This surprised me, but it also felt appropriate.

LM: How have your gifts matured over time?

RSH: I'm not sure I'm the right person to answer this. I'm sure that those around me could have a better handle on how I've changed … or not. That being said, I believe that my horizon of time has expanded. I see that planting and nurturing seeds is very important and I'm more patient about the fruition or harvest. It all doesn't have to happen in "this moment." Looking at how our actions will impact generations seems important and to plan for that long distance future. I am also clearer about who I am, what my footprint is. This has allowed my passion and my ability to take a stand and fight for what I care about to be more fully expressed.

LM: When do you know you've received the call to leadership?

RSH: To receive the call, I think it is necessary to have a deeply rich and mature emotional life. One must feel things deeply, the pleasant with the unpleasant. If we're in touch with our bodies, it becomes harder and harder to ignore the call. I think of it as mission or destiny. There is a moment in people's lives, an event, and the calling comes and they respond.

For me, there was something missing, something I didn't see anyone else stepping up to fill. Why did I "see" it? Emotionally, it felt like it would be a huge loss not to fill that void, for myself, for others, for a discourse. Intellectually, there was an ethic that I had to step up and live. It seemed like the proper or right thing to do. I believe ethics are biological in origin. I experience the call as a felt sense rather than something heard or known. I feel it in the trunk of my body — from the top of my pubic bone to my clavicle. I'm galvanized into taking action from that place.

LM: When do you recognize it in someone else?

RSH: They can't not do what they're doing. There's a focus and passion and energy that appears. Yet somebody could have all that and still not be a leader, not be magnetic, compelling, someone you want to follow. The Japanese word for the difference is kibali — the ability to extend that force, that quality, out so that it touches somebody else, enrolls others and brings them along.

LM: How do you know the call has been answered?

RSH: When other people show up. When they appear. Responses ranging from "Where do I sign up?" to "I think you're full of shit" tell you the call is being answered. People are reacting to you.

LM: What do you as a leader need from others in order to be effective? What roles do you need them to play?

RSH: I need people to be in the same story, to have the same standards, have the same grounding for the future and similar practices. I need them to see that the story is beyond both them and me. It's a requirement that they make a commitment to not only seeing themselves in the story, but producing certain futures, certain results, based on shared standards. It's also important that they acknowledge they need other people around them in order to get the work done, and then, as the story gets filled out, they need to allow others into the story in order to replicate themselves. They have to grow and evolve.

I also need people to tell me when I'm off, people to give me straight feedback. I need to continue to stay in my own practices, in my own discourses — that keeps me honest, keeps me straight, keeps me evolving, gives me perspective.

LM: Describe for me your own leadership journey, please.

I was asked, or as you say "called," into a leadership role. I saw that something was missing and that it was important to bring it into form. No one else was doing it, so I stepped up to the plate. There was a requirement to occupy and be a space, be a provider of a certain kind of learning. This means I had to let go of what was comfortable and known, to go beyond myself. This always seems to have anxiety and fear. It's a death of a certain self to evolve into a larger self. At this point one has to go beyond oneself.

RSH: What do you think is its destination?

Does it end? I have no feeling for what the destination is. I've got a good thirty years ahead of me and I'm putting one foot in front of me while I look to the horizon. But then there's maybe a period of detaching, the interest changes. What happens then? I'm closely studying the one living teacher I have left. It helps me read the world and see what's possible in it. I see that the body changing has a lot to do with what's possible. I'm trying to keep my ear to the track and see what's calling and what's needed.

LM: What gets in the way of your leadership?

RSH: My hankering for comfort gets in the way. Sometimes I just want to lay down in the snow and go to sleep. I also observe myself becoming rigid in the transitions, hanging on to people or to conversations in ways that are inappropriate, and that gets in the way. These are old, conditioned historical conversations that I have to continually monitor.

LM: What are the dilemmas that cause you the greatest concern?

RSH: I struggle to find the balance between the leadership role and the other relationships and responsibilities in my life — my children, my relationships, my wife, the land and the animals.

LM: What have been your most transformational experiences as a leader?

RSH: Seeing the places where I've produced breakdowns — where I've fallen short, broken commitments, made declarations without a ground under them, where I was out of integrity or not accountable. Those things have clearly offered opportunities for transformation and learning. Certain things my teacher has pointed to have been transformational. When these things happen, I'm much more mobilized with velocity, certitude, alignment.

LM: What do you understand about leadership now that you didn't five or ten years ago?

RSH: That there's really a joy in it. That there's a continuity about it, you do it 24/7, but not in a grim, drudgery way. You're open to possibilities. That in some way or another we're in a time which we must all step up to leadership. Leadership as a role or leadership as a way of being.

LM: What's the how of leadership?

RSH: The how of leadership is what Socrates called ethos: how one carries oneself. What is the energetic presence of a leader? How do you comport yourself that generates trust and accountability? We must be the change. When one has the leadership presence, others are compelled to say, "I want to go forward with you."

LM: What's the relevance of leadership today?

RSH: We find ourselves in a time of confusion about the relationship of humans to technology. We're soft and overfed, and we live in entitlement. There's confusion between humans and media; our stories are in bad shape and we're fed so much information that we can be wonderfully informed and never take a stand. It leaves a huge opportunity and opening for reconnecting to the ground of our being. Our humanity is at stake and leaders are called to take a stand for wisdom, compassion, authenticity and courage.

RISING FROM SUCH A DEPTH

V | BEING THE HERO IN OUR OWN STORY

Anyone can slay a dragon, he told me,
but try waking up every morning and
loving the world all over again.
That's what takes a real hero.

~ BRIAN ANDREAS

"But I'm not a hero; I'm just an average person. How can I be a hero?"

It's a natural enough reaction, given that the hero archetype is that of the warrior, taking great personal risk to defeat evil.[76] After all, isn't that what we see in the comics and on TV? No. Those are superheroes, not the heroes I'm talking about. Aren't the majority of the truly heroic acts we hear about performed by perfectly ordinary people, just doing what they thought they should do?

On January 13, 1982, when Air Florida flight 90 crashed into the 14th Street Bridge in downtown Washington, DC, a perfectly ordinary twenty-eight-year-old mail clerk at the Congressional Budget Office named Martin Skutnik, III dove into the icy waters of the Potomac and saved passenger Priscilla Tirado. His sense of what needed to be done to make the world right overshadowed his personal fears.

Similarly, Hugh Thompson, when he saw his fellow soldiers shooting civilians at My Lai, landed his helicopter between the soldiers and ten civilians, ordering his gunner to shoot the soldiers if necessary, while he coaxed the civilians into his aircraft and airlifted them to safety.[77] He never proclaimed his deed, nor was it recognized until decades later.

We must inhabit our own story to the fullest, take the life journey that is our own to take. As David Whyte observed in a speech to the International Coach Federation in 2000, "There is nothing more tragic than living a life only to discover that it was someone else's." To avoid that, one must be the hero of one's own story. In so doing, we each commit to being the best possible version of ourself. With that commitment, we also open ourselves to providing leadership — to ourselves and to others.

Defining the Hero

For our conversation about leadership, I therefore propose this relationship between hero and leader: a hero is someone who rises to the occasion. We should all aspire to be heroes. A leader recognizes the call to be the hero *in her own life*. She aspires to something greater than just getting her own needs met, and answers that call, to fully live her own life and not someone else's.

In our over-blown, over-hyped world, sometimes the fields in which we take ownership for our own lives seem small — raising children, fixing cars, managing projects, driving buses, writing code, working on the assembly line, teaching school, building houses … yet they each offer opportunities to make the world a better place. There are opportunities for small daily heroism *and* for leadership. If we choose to be the hero in our own lives, we will see those opportunities. Then each opportunity is intrinsically a call to leadership.

So a leader will always be a hero, though a hero may not always be a leader. Indeed, for some, that "heroic" response may never result in an active leadership role, although it will surely result in a life lived with integrity. (That is one reason the hero's journey provides such a powerful architecture for leadership development.) For others, it will be a first step in a life of leadership, and for still others it may result in periodic leadership roles.

That call can come in as dramatic a form as the ones described earlier, or in simply recognizing an unmet need in an organization, one's family or in society. For one person, it may simply be a matter of seeing the implied request in a memo and responding in a way that benefits the entire organization. For another, it may be the impulse to give back, to use gifts or return benefits received, which results in a community program that changes people's lives. There are as many examples as there are leaders.

We Are the Ones We Have Been Waiting For

Here is one way to think about leadership and heroism:

> There is a river flowing now very fast. It is so great and swift that there are those who will be afraid. They will try to hold on to the shore. They feel they are being torn apart and will suffer greatly.
>
> Know the river has its destination. The Elders say we must let go of the shore, push off into the middle of the river, keep our eyes open and our heads above the water. And I say, see who is there with you and celebrate.
>
> At this time in history, we are to take nothing personally. Least of all, ourselves. For the moment that we do, our spiritual growth and journey comes to a halt.
>
> The time of the lone wolf is over. Gather yourselves!
>
> Banish the word "struggle" from your attitude and your vocabulary. All that we do now must be done in a sacred manner and in celebration.
>
> *We are the ones we have been waiting for.*[78]

This message speaks deeply to being the hero in our own lives, in our own story. Pushing off from the shore is accepting our call, overcoming fear and giving over to forces more powerful than our own desires. When we "take nothing personally," we don't default to victimhood. We don't focus on the struggle and get trapped in a circle of blaming others or the world or life, thus losing sight of the possibilities in our own story.

"And I say, see who is there with you and celebrate." Heroes today don't work alone. Be grateful, this suggests, for those with whom we work, for those whose stories seek a similar destination to our own. They are companions on the journey. We need them for mental health, as well as to get the work done.

If our story is that of waiting for a leader to appear or waiting to be rescued, be it in our organization, community or personal life, we must give that story up. It is time to become that leader ourselves. Rescue comes from taking one's own journey, in concert with others, in taking responsibility for the outcome of one's own story. Endlessly waiting for someone else to do something, even if they are indeed the designated responsibility-holder, is a way of resigning from one's story. Don't worry about what *they* should do; what can *you* do?

Companions on the Journey

In the great stories, the leaders have companions: Robin Hood, for example, had his band of Merry Men; Odysseus, his Companions; Jason, the Argonauts; Peter Pan had Tinker Bell and the Lost Boys; Harry Potter had Hermione and Ron; and Luke Skywalker had his ragtag band — Yoda, Obi-Wan Kenobi, Princess Leia, Han Solo, Chewbacca, C-3PO and R2-D2. Like so much of the architecture of great stories, this is no accident. We are limbically programmed to need others near us. It is how we physiologically restore ourselves, synchronizing our breathing rates, heartbeats and other life processes to strengthen and amplify ourselves, a phenomenon called "limbic regulation."[79]

Studies done on the failure of infants to thrive when deprived of physical contact with their mothers or caretakers simply reflect a basic physiological reality: biologically, we need connection with other beings. Granted, some people can reregulate themselves with far less connection than others, but all of us need some amount of connection.

Often in the old stories, when the leader begins to distrust and disconnect from his closest supporters (usually through the corrupting force of power), he slips into madness. King Lear is one example. Another is the last years of Alexander the Great, when he alienated old and trusted friends as he sought to be declared a god. That is perhaps an extreme consequence of the loss of limbic regulation, but not an unusual one.

The Merry Many

Beyond satisfying neurological needs, our stories today also unfold in situations of enormous social, economic, political and cultural complexity. The globalization of markets and production has interwoven both patterns of work and patterns of consumption. For example, work on a new computer component design begins in Oregon, is electronically shipped to Malaysia at the end of the day for testing and returns the next morning for more design. "A component may cross a foreign border several times as it moves up the assembly chain into a finished computer, network router or cell phone."[80]

Similarly, the clothes bought at Wal-Mart consist of fabric woven in one country cut to patterns designed in the U.S. and then assembled in Myanmar, Taiwan or elsewhere. Furniture purchased from IKEA may contain parts from as many as twelve countries, all carefully controlled and designed to be assembled in one's living room. Under these conditions, work is simply too complex to have just one leader. While one may lead one's part of the effort, many other leaders need to be doing their part for the whole to work. Leaders, be they First, Second or Third Principle, need the "Merry Many" to accompany them on the journey to make it happen. Who are they?

Archetypes provide a powerful way to understand the Merry Many, the roles people play in a living story. A very useful set of archetypes is described in Carol Pearson's *Awakening the Heroes Within*. While at some point leaders may need all of them, a few key archetypes seem always to be present in the great stories: the Magician, the Trickster, the Outlaw, the Caregiver, the Regular Guy or Gal and the Innocent.

Note that each of these archetypes can also be a leader. Pearson notes that sometimes they are roles played by others, sometimes they are forces within us. As when sandhill cranes fly in formation, no one can be at the front all the time; the job is simply too exhausting. When large birds fly in formation, the lead bird's job is to break up the air, since it is actually easier to fly in turbulence. Behind him, the other birds (the Merry Many) squawk continuous encouragement, and then periodically change positions. It is an apt metaphor for leadership — at all levels. "This is how leaders rest, grow others and compensate for areas of weakness."[81]

Like Yoda in *Star Wars*, the Magician has a powerful connection to the fundamental forces in the universe and plays a visionary role as the story unfolds. This role serves to keep the Merry Many focused on what is possible rather than worrying about what is not possible. The Trickster — like Han Solo — is the guy who breaks the rules and creates the work-arounds that get the job done. While the loyalty of Trickster figures is never one-hundred percent certain, they are absolutely necessary for cobbling together those eleventh-hour solutions that save the day.

The Outlaw, like Darth Vader in *Star Wars*, embodies the Dark Side or shadow side — the organization's energy turned in upon itself: secrecy, repression and even destruction. For example, when divisions or functional areas engage in turf battles or ignore one another instead of working collaboratively for the organization's greater good, the Outlaw force is at play. It is critical that such forces be identified and harnessed. That same energy, if focused outward, can be used to break old ways of thinking and catapult the organization into the next wave of new technologies or services. The leaders need the Outlaw, if only to keep him where he can be watched and that outlaw energy harnessed.

Caregivers may remind you of R2-D2 and C-3PO in *Star Wars*. Their function is to be of service and protect others from harm. They are (ironically, given that they are robots) the limbic resonators, the ones who build much of the team spirit. They will tend to the details and take care of the team, both protecting it and worrying about anyone who does not seem to be thriving. There may be slightly martyrish overtones to this, but they are often the ones providing the emotional glue, making sure there is harmony. Similarly, there need to be Regular Guys & Gals, like Chewbacca, the Wookie, doing much of the heavy lifting so the job gets done. With those folks, there's no pretense, and even if they are not particularly articulate, they are hard-working, supportive and eager to belong to a worthwhile cause.

The Innocent represents purity, the best of what the organization or the project has to offer, or what may be at risk if the project fails.[82] By embodying the espoused values of the effort or the group, the Innocent inspires the rest to be more consistent in their practicing of those values. In doing so, the Innocent provides a kind of moral compass, a sense of "true north" that helps people stay on track. Again drawing on the *Star Wars* story, Princess Leia offers a good example of the Innocent role.

With these archetypal forces in play, leaders are far better equipped to handle the kinds of complexity, ambiguity and paradox inherent in leading today. The way the roles play out is also impacted by whether the situation calls for heroic, collaborative or dialogic leaders — Drath's First, Second and Third Principles. The Magician helps the Merry Many see what is possible (and keep people believing in it), the Innocent helps hold the moral center, the Trickster finds ways around obstacles, the Outlaw promotes out-of-the-box thinking, the Caregivers keep everyone supported and the Regular Guys & Gals do the heavy lifting. Each one has a call to respond to, and each builds the overall organizational gestalt or culture.

Peter Pan Leadership

That leadership can no longer be accomplished alone is actually old news. There is no question that thirty years of "right-sizing" and re-engineering, along with globalization and the impact of the Internet, have left little room for Lone Rangers if real work is to get done. (This still often feels counterintuitive, however, in a culture that reveres Batman and Superman as the ultimate heroes and consistently rewards individual rather than team contributions.) The leadership role needs to change even further.

In the U.S. today, the archetypal model for leadership is essentially the model of Peter Pan. Peter Pan leadership is that of the charismatic, youthful leader who cares only for his Lost Boys and for playing and winning — leadership that refuses to grow up. The romantic hero who dies young is a variation on this theme, since he or she stays enshrined in our memory as a youth. Charismatic figures, people who attract others to them, make their world seem more enticing than our own, be it more productive, more successful, filled with better adventures or in some other way more attractive.

Peter Pan adamantly refuses to remember the past and grow from it, which allows him to play the same games endlessly and still find them fascinating. There is little or no growth or maturing required in order to achieve and maintain leader status in Peter Pan leadership. Psychologists refer to this as the *puer aeternis*, the eternal youth. Carl Jung, the first psychologist to have deeply studied archetypes, is said to have commented that the twentieth century would be dominated by the *puer aeternis*, reaching its apex in the last part of the century. The rise of the dot-com era in the United States certainly fits within that prophecy, as do unhappy circumstances like China's Cultural Revolution and the boy soldiers currently fighting in parts of West Africa.

The cultural roots of this model probably go back through Norse culture to an even older Germanic warrior code:

> The prospect of gaining a glorious name in the *wael-raes* (the rush of battle-slaughter), the pride of defending one's lord and bearing heroic witness to the integrity of the bond between him and his hall-companions — a bond sealed in the *gleo* and *gidd* of peacetime feasting and ring-giving — this is what gave drive and sanction to the Germanic warrior-culture enshrined in *Beowulf*.[83]

This version of heroism and leadership was carried south to Scotland and Ireland during the Norse invasions of the ninth & tenth centuries. The Vikings' path to Valhalla, the afterlife, was through having the "best death" — the one that would be talked about for the longest time.

> For every one of us, living in this world
> Means waiting for our end. Let whoever can
> Win glory before death. When a warrior is gone,
> That will be his best and only bulwark.[84]

These same beliefs ultimately became embedded in the Scottish Highlands culture as part of the clan system.

In what was essentially a nasty, brutish (and usually short) lifetime, clan members made what meaning they could by glorifying deeds of violence, and an early death was an honorable one. No one bothered to "grow up," even if life afforded the chance. It is the same simple system of "might makes right" practiced by warlords in the Balkans, Afghanistan and Ethiopia as well as the drug lords of Central America and crime bosses and gang leaders in our cities today. Wordsworth captured its essence in his poem about Rob Roy:

For why? Because the good old rule
    Sufficeth them; the simple plan,
That they should take who have the power,
    And they should keep who can....
"Since then," said Robin, "right is plain,
    And longest life is but a day,
To have my ends, maintain my rights,
    I'll take the shortest way."[85]

This sounds similar to the positions taken today by business chieftains such as Bill Gates, Larry Ellison and Steve Jobs, who exult in a ruthlessly competitive approach to all they do.

Further romanticized by Sir Walter Scott in the early eighteenth century, the "noble" Scottish clan chieftain became a potent leadership model throughout the southern United States as immigration to that part of the country effectively ceased after the Scottish Highland migrations of the 1700s and very early 1800s. More than any other part of the United States, the South developed family histories that emphasized family (tribal) connections, a romantic past and a fervent attachment to a lost cause, similar to Scottish passions for Bonnie Prince Charlie once he was gone. (Interestingly enough, *Peter Pan* was written in 1911 by a Scotsman, James M. Barrie.)

To this day, the South sends a disproportionate number of young men into military service,[86] which in turn trains them rigorously in the First Principle's warrior code leadership that easily slips into Peter Pan.[87] (While age and maturity are clearly not synonymous, an institution that is populated primarily by people in their twenties, and whose senior leadership for the most part is in its forties, is limited in its capacity to develop and sustain collaborative — Principle Two — or dialogic — Principle Three — leadership.) In turn, "The military is, in fact, an institution that many high-tech and New Economy companies use for their leadership models."[88]

Peter Pan was arguably the dominant management model of the 1990s, as the dot-com's so-called "New Economy" took hold in Silicon Valley and spread. Youth, adventure, fun and games were themes sounded constantly by the business press, the sports press and venture capitalists. Now, as it becomes clear that the New Economy was not any newer than the Dutch tulip mania a few hundred years earlier, the costs of having adopted this model are becoming clear.

Breaking the Peter Pan Syndrome

Thoughtful and competent leaders who recognize the flaws in the Peter Pan model, with its focus on youth, conquest and dominance, still struggle to identify an effective replacement. Again, the stories we are told about leaders today, in the media and in our leadership development training, are in severe disrepair, insufficient for the world we face. We do not talk about the end point when we discuss the growth and development of leaders. We do not have maturity models for leadership. Nor do we often tell stories about young leaders who grow old and wise or become elder statesmen. In the U.S., especially in recent decades, we have idolized youthful leaders, condoning (indeed, encouraging) their Peter Pan-like refusal to grow up.

Other cultures, especially the so-called primitive cultures, do not always display this absence of maturity models. For example, in the Masai tribe, young men in their late teens are circumcised and initiated into warriorhood. A decade or so later, another ritual ceremony called "Eunoto" moves them *beyond* warriorhood into elderhood. At the end of Eunoto, senior elders advise them, "Now that you are an elder, drop your weapons and use your head and wisdom instead."[89]

Perhaps one aspect of the Peter Pan dilemma is that the dialogue around leadership has been framed in a binary, *either/or* way. Either a person is youthful and charismatic or not — and if the latter is true, that person cannot be a leader. For most of us, no clear alternative emerges. What we need instead is, at minimum, a *both/and* model, in which there are developmental stages, each of which includes and transcends the previous stage.

Warriorhood since the Industrial Revolution seems to have been split between the military (those with "the right stuff") and the business world (e.g. "corporate raiders"). Recently, it has appeared as fast-tracking MBAs or dot-com CEO roles, athletic superstars, venture capitalists and corporate raiders or turn-around artists. The Michael Dells, Larry Ellisons, Barry Bondses and Michel Jordans of the world receive disproportionate amounts of media attention, with few competing models.

Missing in the conversation on leadership is this question: is that the best we can do? And beyond that conversation lies another, one people seem reluctant to have — the conversation about elderhood. There are few currently known models for elderhood; it is simply not a state commanding respect. Indeed, it has become commonplace in business to pay those who might be our elders to leave the organization through buyouts and early retirement packages. The message is that they are unnecessary. Similarly, the phrase "elder statesman" has almost totally lost its currency.

There are two current leadership conversations that do hold potential for elderhood in the leadership domain. One is Robert Greenleaf's "Servant Leadership" concept, developed in the 1970s. Greenleaf focused on those who became leaders out of a desire to serve others. He set a high standard:

> The best test, and difficult to administer, is: Do those served grow as persons; do they, while being served, become healthier, wiser, freer, more autonomous, more likely themselves to become servants? And what is the effect on the least privileged in society; will they benefit, or, at least, will they not be further deprived?[90]

Obviously, such a standard requires a high level of self-awareness and maturity to put into effect. There has been little conversation, however, about the developmental progression one might go through to become a servant leader.

The other conversation is the Noel Tichy/Jack Welch "leader as teacher" approach, reflected in Tichy's book *The Leadership Engine*. While the book does take the importance of story into consideration, and provides a "Handbook for Leaders Developing Leaders," it, too, fails to offer a developmental path.

Conclusion: Be the Leader in Your Own Life

If we complain about the lack of leadership in our lives, we must recognize it is up to us to provide that leadership. We must start by being the heroes in our own stories. To do that, each one of us needs the Merry Many, the archetypal companions on our journey who will keep us mentally healthy and morally directed. Further, we need to be alert to the seductive pull of Peter Pan, the leadership syndrome that requires us *not* to mature.

David Whyte points out, as I've said earlier, "We don't have language commensurate with the world we are entering." That language will only develop when conversations for sense-making about leadership are started, when the right questions are asked and the shared understanding developed. Those include conversations about the leadership journey and how others have gotten from point A to points B and C and D, from Peter Pan to elderhood. What might a logical developmental process look like? How might we assess ourselves along a continuum if we wanted to become a mature leader someday?

The hero's journey offers some clues.

CONVERSATION

KNOW ME BY MY FRUITS
ROBERT DILTS OF ISVOR-DILTS

Robert Dilts has consulted and trained on leadership and organizational development throughout the world for over twenty-five years. Clients include Apple Computer, Hewlett-Packard, IBM, the World Bank, Alitalia, Telecom Italia, Lucasfilms Ltd., Ernst & Young and the State Railway of Italy. He has lectured extensively on leadership, organizational learning and change management, making presentations and keynote addresses for The European Forum for Quality Management, the World Health Organization and Harvard University. Robert has worked with Fiat since 1988, helping to develop programs on leadership, innovation, values and systemic thinking.

*Robert has authored or coauthored over fifteen books as well as numerous articles, including most recently, **Alpha Leadership: Tools for Business Leaders Who Want More from Life** (with Anne Deering and Julian Russell). Robert was one of the developers of NeuroLinguistic Programming (NLP), a powerful way of understanding how people take in and process information, and has been founder or CEO of several other venture capital and behavioral engineering companies. He has a degree in Behavioral Technology from the University of California at Santa Cruz.*

Robert is a person of both great intellect and great integrity. His ability to scale from the micro — the tiniest steps of a behavioral change process — to the macro — as in exploring the neurological and thought processes that create health — is extraordinary. His definition of leadership, which emerged in the earliest days of his work at Fiat, is one that has informed my thinking throughout this book. Robert really deepens the conversation about the meaning of

| 75 |

leadership. He also foreshadows much of what is to come, in terms of the nature of the leadership journey, some of the issues (monsters) that must be confronted and how profoundly different it makes us at the end of the journey.

LISA MARSHALL: Robert, I know you have also been using Joseph Campbell's hero's journey as well as NeuroLinguistic Programming in your work with organizations. How do you define leadership these days?

ROBERT DILTS: I've found it useful to look at the etymological roots of the word "leader." It comes from the Old English word *lithan*, which means "to go, to travel." Thus leadership really means to cause to go, to make go, not to command or coerce. It doesn't mean status, command, power; it's going, making something go. That is the deep structure that is still the source of leadership.

Some useful leadership distinctions that I use are:

- **micro** leadership means organizing the task and the team to reach the goal;
- **macro** leadership means building culture, establishing values, developing strategy; and
- **meta** leadership means vision-based leadership, setting a direction.

Meta leadership, for me, is associated with charisma. Genuine charisma comes from congruence, alignment with something larger than you. I also like to make a distinction between the *cult of the leader* versus the *culture of leadership*. What you describe as *presence*, Lisa, may be the awakening of others' sense of their power by the leader. To me, it's leading by example instead of being the source of power, or external reference instead of internal reference. When the leader is the reference, you have a cult.

I still think the best definition is "Creating a world that people want to belong in and to which they can contribute." People's desire to belong is embedded in their being able to contribute. Leaders create the conditions under which others can win, can thrive. Today leaders have to lead other leaders in the areas where leadership is most necessary, where there's lots of change and challenge. Creating the conditions under which others can have their own vision and align it to the bigger picture — that's meta leadership.

The other way I define it has four elements or dimensions:

- **self** (internal congruency, being an example, the role model);
- **others** (requires communication, understanding, motivation — you can't lead someone you don't understand; you can command, coerce or punish);
- **goals** (vision, path); and
- **systems** (stakeholders, including environment, values, mission).

Note that mission is in relationship to something outside you, not your identity. It comes from the Latin "missio," "to be sent." What are you sent to accomplish? Leadership is about managing all those things. We need multiple models of leadership, and they need to include those same dynamics.

LM: What, in your mind, is the internal drive to lead?

RD: Leadership is a consequence of wanting to improve, to change the context, having a desired state and the will to go there, to go somewhere new. Management is trying to optimize the present; leadership is going somewhere new. The felt need for leadership has increased dramatically because we're in the unknown.

LM: What do you think is its source?

RD: The source of that drive is your vision and calling. There's a call — to action or being. There's a call to change, to grow. The source is something within you — in relation to something outside of you. A calling has a relationship between you and the system. Sometimes vision is more self-generated. When you are called, the environment calls upon you.

Some people can resist the call pretty effectively. Calling has to do with your self and your own internal preparation. Sometimes you're called away from, rather than toward. And, by being in an environment of low change, you're less likely to be called. At the edge, there's more frontier, more opportunity to get a call.

You need a threshold of capability. As you grow internally, suddenly there is a place where you can apply that new or increased capability. So part of the source of the impulse to lead is also an awareness, a surveillance, an awakening to capability that goes along with it.

Another way to talk about it is whether you are leading with the brain and pencil or the heart and gut. The real vision is independent of you; you have to figure out "What's my specific role in that?" What is your core contribution? The desire to contribute is a big driver in leadership, a meta-program of leadership. Any time I personally stepped up to, took a leadership role, it was first where I wanted to go and then my belief that I could do it. Leadership is going first.

LM: What was your first experience of your ability to lead?

RD: The experience I can remember where I had the most conscious awareness of taking a leadership role, one which has played out dynamically in lots of ways since then, was being in Scouts. I wasn't a social leader, however I remember that at Jamboree, no one else had the competence to do the things that we were supposed to do. I did; I knew what to do. It wasn't an issue of power. My leadership came because I could show them how to do it. I wasn't the biggest, the fastest, couldn't bully or be the alpha male, but I could communicate, I somehow knew what was needed to organize a team to get to a result. I knew how to collaborate, along with having some technical knowledge and a degree of proactivity.

That experience still shapes my own views, explains why I don't think of leadership as hierarchical or power-based, but as drawing on the credibility or authority that comes from competence. Self-confidence is needed; you have to believe you can do it. There is the situation, and there is your ability.

LM: When do you know you've received the call to leadership?

RD: "Knowledge is only a rumor until it's in the muscle" is a proverb from New Guinea. I think it's true of leadership; it's only a rumor until it's in the muscle, until you can act on it. Leadership means to go, to act, to move. What moves you into action? That is your call.

LM: When and how do you recognize it in someone else?

RD: Is there action? That's the test. Some people only know what isn't right, not what is, so there's also a kind of call to action that comes from reactivity. There's another that comes from proactivity.

Ultimately, it's spiritual, a commitment to something larger than yourself. We've noticed in our work at Fiat that the great leaders there all had a commitment to the social responsibility and activity of the company. Meta leadership is not only about motivating other leaders, but also creating, sponsoring, awakening leadership. Succession-planning raises these issues. You have to create a path of experiences to develop this maturity.

LM: How do you know the call has been answered?

RD: When I think about how I know the call's been answered, I'm reminded of the biblical phrase "Know me by my fruits." All leadership is ultimately results-related in some way. I've found that modeling (studying in detail how people get the results they get), based on benchmarks, is powerful for both assessing and teaching leadership. One of the key issues in assessing leadership is time. To institutionalize a leadership culture, you have to plan for the long term and build a leadership team. I've never led alone; it's always as part of a team.

LM: What do you as a leader need from others in order to be effective? What roles do you need them to play?

RD: Campbell talks about heroes needing guardians, those archetypal figures that provide sponsorship and mentoring along the journey. Their support is what helps us build skills, believe in ourselves and stay focused on the journey. For myself, what I need from others depends on the circumstances, the logical levels at which the situation is operating. I need more or less depending on my competencies, how much I've grown in a given domain.

I also need shared values, and then there are roles I need people to play; that's the archetypal aspect. I need somebody at the fundamental levels of dreamer, realist and critic. In challenging times, the leader has to be the realist role. They need the dreamer to remind them of what it is they're trying to do. The critic keeps me in touch with the common person, the lowest common denominator.

I'm one of the ones who gets called a lot. This is why you need a team; you can't accomplish much by yourself. The shift from hero to leader is important; not all heroes are leaders. And not all leaders are heroes. The transformation is from hero to a team.

LM: Describe your own leadership journey.

RD: It's a journey of discovery. As an Irish Catholic, I was exposed to the stories of Jesus, the touchstone of all leadership in the Western framework. In that story, Jesus was a reluctant leader, whose leadership was discovered or brought out in interactions with key others who weren't necessarily key mentors. You can read it as a whole series of awakenings. John the Baptist says something about him, gets arrested, Jesus has to flee, meets the woman at the well who reminds him of his calling. That's an awakening. Then he runs into a nobleman who asks him to heal his son. Jesus doesn't want to, but does it out of the congruence, the alignment of his person, and his ability is again awakened.

That pattern reflects something in my personal leadership journey. My awakenings come sometimes in non-obvious interactions, and almost always come from others. I've noticed that the awakening to a bigger calling comes from little callings.

My whole involvement in NLP is a big part of my story. That had a lot to do with taking a risk, making a commitment. Like Campbell says, you have a calling and you cross a threshold, the frontier outside your comfort zone into which you must step, and which constitutes a point of no return. You have to ask: "If not us, who? If not now, when?" My own journey has been a lot of moments like that.

Personal awakenings take you to the change moment, the place where you confront who you are, not in reference to others but to yourself. There's a certain point where the only motivation to go on is internal. Most actions of genius weren't for external reward. I think the change moment is discovering the essence of yourself: what would you still do if you were locked in a prison for twenty years?

For me, many of the significant decision moments required thinking about my own inner truth; otherwise, if you don't, you get depressed. The demon of depression teaches the hero to find him- or herself, find the ground of meaning inside of you.

LM: What is the destination?

RD: "Leader" doesn't mean "arrive at," it means "to go." So it's about the journey and not the destination. The ultimate goal is to leave things better than you found them — somewhere in between what it used to be and what it could be. That's the common thing that vital and lively old people say: it's not about achieving, it's about moving. I see a lot of heroes that haven't returned home.

LM: What gets in the way of your leadership?

RD: Two things get in my way. The most common is my confrontation with time and availability. It's as though there were a Peter Principle of leadership. You expand to fill the available time and then you start having lapses, not out of laziness or incompetence, but just because there are so many demands. You've got to prioritize. The calling is not just your goal, it's that people are calling you. It is easy to miss what is important but not urgent. It's like juggling; you drop a ball every once in a while.

The second: Carlos Castaneda says you overcome fear with power, and then power becomes the obstacle, and you have to overcome power with clarity and then clarity becomes the obstacle, and you have to overcome it with letting go. That's a common complaint in most companies: top management doesn't want to let go. When you can let go, there's an incredible sense of freedom. Then you have the re-mission. You let go of the old mission and have to find a new mission. That's a new awakening, a reawakening.

LM: What are the dilemmas that cause you the greatest concern?

RD: For me, the biggest dilemma is determining when do you stand alone and when do you stand together? It's about when to go first and when to go with others, when to empower and when to pioneer. Another one of the big dilemmas is when to let go of others, realizing that "Where I'm going, you cannot come." There have been times when people who had been my teammate, my partner, my soul mate stopped growing, couldn't follow. Recognizing that they aren't going with you any more, that's hard. Similarly, the big dilemma of any downturn is "Who do I let go?"

LM: What have been your most transformational experiences as a leader?

RD: For me, it's those moments — and they're always in a group — when you realize you're responding in a way that you could never have imagined, maybe you didn't know you knew it, or maybe you didn't even know it. That's an awakening experience that's drawn out by the whole convergence of all these factors we've been talking about. Reality has just changed, a miracle has happened, the edge of reality has been punctured, you're breaking the barrier and there's no ego, it's not about you, or because of you, you're a participant (though your calling may have been a precipitating experience). You notice it afterward by what has changed.

In my own life, it might be a dramatic physical healing in the health work I do or in a company where you're doing something no one thought you could. Transformation within is the feeling of growing or expanding, but it's always with others. You *all* get bigger.

LM: What do you understand about leadership now that you didn't five or ten years ago?

RD: Niels Bohr makes a distinction between the shallow truth (where the opposite is false) and the deep truth (where the opposite is also true). I understand more about those challenges, those realities of leadership. I understand a lot more about the higher levels of leadership. Ten years ago I was focusing on the skills of leadership. Now I understand the reality of mission, vision, and values. You're larger as a leader — and also irrelevant. To describe it sounds like a bunch of paradoxes, yet those are the deeper realities. I have much more empathy for people in leadership positions. And

I understand that all the dimensions are required. The macro and meta leadership. Ten years ago I was focused on the micro.

LM: How have you evolved or matured?

RD: How you evolve is through your failures. When times are tough, you find out what you really believe. It's trial by fire. I've seen it in our research as well: the downturn lets the chaff fall away. And I'm still like a child, believing in the impossible dream. I want to keep that.

If you're not afraid, you don't need courage. The change points are where there's anxiety and risk, and you summon courage, acknowledge the danger and face it.

THE PIT

THE CURRENTS OF THE GREAT DESIRE
VI
THE PULL OF THE PIT

> *Original experience has not been interpreted for you, and so you've got to work out your life for yourself. Either you can take it or you can't. You don't have to go far off the interpreted path to find yourself in very difficult situations. The courage to face the trials and to bring a whole new body of possibilities into the field of interpreted experience for other people to experience — that is the hero's deed.*
>
> ~ JOSEPH CAMPBELL[91]

The journey is the story. It is the adventure of working out our lives, living our stories and accepting our leadership role. The journey includes our steps along the path, our forward movement and our choice to stay stuck, circle back or spiral upward. The milestones we plan are the external manifestations of the story; the deeper structure lies in the internal work we do to survive and grow inside the story. The story includes our entry into what Campbell called "the pit," the places of adversity we encounter in reaching those milestones. How we respond to the enemies and allies encountered along the way, and the way we change over time before reaching home are the core of each of our stories.

In a great story, the main character ultimately returns home, the same but different. In entering the pit and facing her monsters, she has brought forth new possibilities, discovered new things about her capacities, her gifts and herself. And now she has gifts to return, to give back to the world. The journey is taking the path to greater leadership in all aspects of a person's life. That is the hero's work.

The journey is ultimately about *choices*: the choice to heed the call, the choice to leave the familiar and start out, the choice of path (and pit), the choice of response when encountering monsters, the choices about what to hold fast to (values) and what to let go of in order to return safely home, and, finally, the choice to give back to the world. Maturing represents development, both in how to frame those choices and in the distinctions that illuminate whether the choices are good and the path the right one.

Our Living Story

In this book we have referred to the journey as the living story, a story whose goal is "to fulfill its potential and to become as great as it can be."[92] A person's living story as a leader is also about fulfilling his potential and answering the greatness within. It takes into account the past, the present and the future, expressing his identity as it evolves the current reality, and his hopes and aspirations.

As noted earlier, if someone's story is not told, over and over, until it is completely familiar, it can be dismissed as a fluke, a fable or wishful thinking. Telling it moves it from rumor to muscle. This is critical: if it is not told and retold, if it does not become part of the lore of the organization, the family, the culture or the self, a story can never take hold and become reality. In fact, it is quite likely to be supplanted by another story that represents something closer to the "path of least resistance."

When told often and well, a living story gets woven into the fabric of both collective and individual leadership identities, becoming the basis for yet more possibilities. In the United States, the story that it is a "land of opportunity" has given generations of immigrants and their children hope for a better life. That hope has in turn translated into one of the key drivers of the economy — the small business person. If such a story were not told over and over, it would not move from rumor or fable to muscle and economic success for succeeding waves of immigrants, again and again. Similarly, the stories we tell ourselves about our identity — that we are winners or losers, for example — play out quite directly in our lives.

At the same time, we need to be cautious about where and when we tell a new story about ourselves or our organization. Told to cynical or resistant audiences, a new story can wither under the blast of hostile or untrusting responses. We want to tell a new story first in safe places, where hearing the words aloud can serve to strengthen and reinforce. This does not mean avoiding good critical thinking, just those people whose fearfulness, cynicism or caustic natures will cause new shoots to wither before they have had a chance to gain strength and resilience.

The rare successful merger, when examined closely, unfolds as a story first told cautiously amongst a select few, and then told more and more widely, until everyone in the organization could see, hear, smell, taste and feel that the story was theirs. Likewise, successfully effecting a behavior change, such as becoming punctual, must be told first to a few close friends and then, as the "muscle" develops, more widely announced.

Finding Our Own Living Story

To thrive, the living story must also be a story of living with the questions, learning to prolong what William Bridges calls the "Neutral Zone,"[93] the period when all things are possible, rather than seeking the quick fix or locking onto the first answer to allay anxiety. For some, this may be akin to a decision to stay in the pit. However, it has great benefits. Indeed, a living story includes asking essential questions, discovering new possibilities and redirecting energies. It faces forward instead of merely gathering data, seeking consensus or dwelling in inertia. A living story does not, however, rush to reach the end, to get there, to finish. The journey *is* the story.

The story also supports the hard work of becoming self-differentiated as a leader, strong enough so as not to be swayed by other people's fears, nor afraid to lead.[94] As a leader, through holding clear boundaries, containing our anxiety and often creating provisional structures, we provide structure for those we are leading, enabling them to get work done and exert their own leadership.

Presence: Moving Past Charisma

Ultimately, the destination of a person's living story is her maturity. It is about coming into her "bigness," accepting fully the unique possibilities she represents, and, at the same time, understanding that every choice she makes represents the narrowing of other kinds of possibilities. Every living story of mature leadership is a story of a leader who faces reality — the pit — unflinchingly, and in doing so, gains wisdom, grows up. Florence Nightingale, who, when she realized that the lack of sanitation in her own hospital was the cause of thousands of deaths in the Crimean War, still wanted the news published so that conditions would change in the future, is an excellent example.

In today's world, Nelson Mandela's remarkable ability to lead South Africa through its transition to the enfranchisement of the majority population is an extraordinary illustration of such a leader. By not playing the "blame game," and at the same time supporting the efforts to get people to tell the truth about the past, Mandela did indeed provide leadership that spoke the truth and pointed to hope. Warren Buffet, Vaclav Havel, the playwright-president of Czechoslovakia, and Jimmy Carter (post-Presidency) are other examples that come to mind.

These mature leaders are people who have moved past charisma, the ability to attract people, to "presence," used here as the ability to enlarge people. Much of how the mature leader leads is through such presence, rather than actions. Whether action is required or meaning must first be made, when leadership presence enlarges the people around the leader and the outcomes have been clearly communicated, people rise to the occasion and perform superbly. As one former Strategic Business Unit president at EDS said about his own growth, "Fundamental was a willingness to surrender self-recognition for the group's recognition. If you don't care who gets the credit, you can accomplish ANYTHING!"[95] This is an illustration of mature leadership, when the people can say, "We did it ourselves."

So what is that quality I am calling presence? Presence in a leader is the quality of a contained self, comfortable in its own skin, a self that does not lose connection with its purpose, with truth and with other people. In that way, the leader's bearing, her way of carrying or conducting herself, creates the incentive and the space for others to be exactly who they are, and, at the same time, invites them to discover their own presence and their larger selves.

Presence also means that both an active heart and an active mind are fully present, alive in the moment. Only when the leader's heart is as powerful as his intellect will people sense a strong leadership presence and voluntarily respond. Presence is the tie between leadership and the capacity for love.

Through the power of such presence, people come to believe in themselves enough to do it themselves. This is precisely the impact of a great community organizer. Whether he works with tenant farmers or aerospace engineers, is a great teacher (as Tichy and Welsh maintain), becomes a great servant-leader (à la Greenleaf) or a great CEO (according to Jim Collins), the people always recognize they did it themselves. It is the mark of real greatness in leadership.

Bill Rauch was one of twenty winners in 2001 of the *Leadership for a Changing World* competition, sponsored by the Ford Foundation and others. As a co-founder of Cornerstone Theater, he uses amateur theater as "a rehearsal for changing the world" by addressing community issues — difficult issues, such as an AIDS initiative in rural Virginia, school segregation in Mississippi, racial profiling in Los Angeles or unwed mothers in Oregon. He notes, "I am moved to make plays with the majority of our population who claim they have no stories to tell because I have learned that they always do."[96]

This deep belief in what others are capable of helps create presence. Whether one is redesigning work flow for a global chip manufacturer, teaching civics in high school or getting grassroots people to ask for a traffic light so their children can safely cross a busy street, this quality of presence allows everyone to take ownership and contribute fully to what needs to be done.

One of the most powerful moments in any living story occurs when a profound connection ignites between the leader's presence and the people's story. This is limbic resonance at its finest, a kind of amplifying of ability for the leader to both be the story and contain the story, not just talk about it. With that level of clarity and compassion, with defined boundaries and connection, people enlarge into and act as their best selves. This is a leader about whom the people say, "We did it ourselves." Leadership at that point is not simply a function of being in front of everyone. It can come from anywhere in the room, because it is through the leader's presence, not positional authority, that forward motion is enabled.

Liz Lerman, a dancer, choreographer and teacher who received a MacArthur "genius grant" in 2002 for her work in "redefining where dance takes place and who can dance,"[97] is one leader who has figured out how to systematically create that limbic resonance. With her powerful vision that all people are capable of dance, she has helped shipyard workers, ministers, people in retirement homes and many others create and perform community-building performances that combine dance, music and the spoken word to share insights and build connections.

Taking the Journey: Traveling Through the "Wormhole"

In Pfeffer and Sutton's book, *The Knowing-Doing Gap*, the authors observe that, in the business and media world, people who are cynical are perceived as smarter than others. Similarly, optimistic people are seen as naïve, and perhaps not as bright.[98] Yet, no matter what a person's earlier stances in life have been, becoming a great leader requires a return to optimism. If a would-be leader does not believe that the seemingly impossible is in fact possible, her leadership is implicitly limited, as is her personal development.

In the transition from Peter Pan leadership to elderhood or mature leadership, a person must move beyond well-developed cynicism to understanding the twin powers of hope and truth. In many science fiction books and films, when the hero experiences a dramatic shift in physical reality, such as being moved into a different dimension, the experience is often described as *going through the wormhole.*[99] Scientists explain a wormhole as:

> … a tunnel between two different locations in space. Light rays from A to B can enter one mouth of the wormhole, pass through the throat and exit at the other mouth — a journey that would take much longer if they had to go the long way around.[100]

This metaphor of time travel, of a somewhat unpredictable shortcut to a profoundly different world, is often mirrored in stories of leadership development. The wormhole experience is often a way of exiting the pit. In the story that follows, the wormhole engenders a clear move toward elderhood. The leadership journey may hold a similar experience for everyone.

Moving to Elderhood

Mort Meyerson, former CEO of EDS, wrote an article called "Everything I Thought I Knew about Leadership Was Wrong" after he became CEO of Perot Systems in 1996. For him, the wormhole involved abandoning the rigid "I win, you lose" mentality that had dominated his thinking at EDS. Meyerson's story is one of metamorphosis from a First Principle leader to a Third Principle leader, one who supports the meaning-making processes so that the right questions are asked, and others can then make the right decisions. The story illuminates the nature of the shift required for reaching elderhood in leadership. He comments:

> There's a much larger calling in business today than was allowed by the old definitions of winning and losing. One hundred years from now, we'll know we were on the right track if there are more organizations where people are doing great work for their customers and creating value for their shareholders. And raising these children, nurturing their families and taking an interest in their communities. And feeling proud of the contributions they make. These are things one can't measure when winning and losing are the only financial metrics.

> It's taken me a while to learn these things. When I returned to Perot Systems, my first job as a leader was to create a new understanding of myself. I had to accept the shattering of my own self-confidence. I couldn't lead anymore, at least not in the way I always had. There was a time during that first year at Perot Systems when I would go home and look in the mirror and say to myself, "You don't get it. Maybe you ought to get out of this business. You're like a highly specialized, trained beast that evolved during one period and now can't adjust to the new environment."

> I told myself I was having the same experience as a caterpillar entering a cocoon. The caterpillar doesn't know that he'll come out as a butterfly. All he knows is that he's alone, its dark and it's a little scary. I came out the other end of the experience with a new understanding of leadership. I don't have to know everything. I don't have to have all the customer contacts. I don't have to make all the decisions. In fact, in the new world of business, it *can't* be me, it *shouldn't* be me, and my job is to prevent it from being me.[101]

Meyerson redefined the metrics for success and then had to do the difficult, scary work of aligning his behavior with his understanding — moving himself out of the pit. His experiences are not unique to those who do the hard work of gaining maturity.

Conclusion: The Path to a Great Story

Our journey is our leadership story, the sum of all the choices we make about responding to our call, taking risks, listening to our heart and mind as we follow our path, fall into our pits, face our monsters and return. It is a living story, and as such, must be told well and cautiously, sensitive to the power that negative listening can have in its early stages. Discovering the full richness of that story also requires listening to ourselves and the world to discover what wants to happen. It requires experiencing the story as it unfolds, not rushing it to a conclusion that cuts short on the promise simply because we can't stand being in the pit, experiencing the anxiety of not knowing what will happen.

If our living leadership story is to be a great story, then it must be, like Mort Meyerson's, a story about maturing, about growing into the kind of presence that enlarges and enables all those around. In doing so we change, become a different person, different in that we are more mature, but the same in that our core identity does not disappear. Such growth and development requires entering the pit and facing our personal "stuff," the things we fear and avoid.

How we face those deepest fears — our "monsters" — forms the basis for the change process at the heart of every great story.

STEWARDSHIP OF THE WHOLE
VICE ADMIRAL JOE DYER, US NAVY, RETIRED
NAVAL AIR SYSTEMS COMMAND (NAVAIR)

Vice Admiral Joseph W. Dyer, US Navy, Retired, was the Commander of the Naval Air Systems Command (NAVAIR). As such, he led the research, development, test, evaluation, procurement and logistics activities for U.S. Navy and U.S. Marine Corps aircraft and air-launched weapons. He grew up in the Smoky Mountains of western North Carolina and has been a government leader in transitioning organizations from functional alignment to integrated program teams. He is a test pilot, an engineer and an organizational developer with a keen interest in people and the things they can accomplish.

Joe is also a maverick, an out-of-the box thinker, a human being with vast curiosity. I put this conversation here not so much because of what he has to say about the leadership journey as much as what he says about leadership being available to everybody, an attitude I found to be unique to people in the military and women. (The rest of the male world tends to think it's a much more genetic or ingrained trait.) Joe's observation that "leadership is stewardship of the whole, not ownership of the parts" is a brilliant discriminator between leaders and managers. And his candid closing observation on the costs of leadership is worth thinking about.

LISA MARSHALL: Joe, you and I share a common fascination with the tough and subtle questions of leadership — what it is and how it works. And I know you have had the experience of leading at multiple scales — 300 people, 3000 people, 30,000 people. So, what definition of leadership do you use?

JOE DYER: A leader is one who has followers. That's not as trivial as I first jokingly offered it. Why *do* people follow one person and not another? Is it genetic, environmental, or can you teach it? I'm a chemical engineer by undergraduate training. That's a very empirical training, which is why I stand by the answer. There's that old line about "Leaders do the right things, managers do things right." Well, you and I have both talked about how not all leaders do the right things. But they do all have to have followers.

I think there are two things required to lead today, and by the way, I'm talking about leading in a network, as opposed to a hierarchy. That's a direct function of the information technology support that goes throughout our world today. First, we're in a technical business at NAVAIR, and I want someone with a technical conscience. That means technical understanding *and* the courage to stand by it, as well as an understanding of the role we play in the sanctity of life. Second is a tremendous tolerance of ambiguity — that is absolutely required. That's almost a first cut for me in leadership selection. Without it, the other choice is misery on both sides. I'm not sure you can train that one.

If you can develop yourself to be the one who says, "Here's a way ahead, here's a way out of the forty years in the wilderness," and do it with conviction and grounding, that's also part of leadership. As we say in the Navy, "You have to have a star to steer by."

LM: What is the internal drive to lead? What is its source?

JD: My colleague Susan Keen notes, "Those of us who see the world as systems and systems of systems are blessed and cursed." One of the compelling underlying drives of leadership is *the refusal to see anything in isolation*. Some of that is trainable. For me, that was the power of an education in chemical engineering (CE); it forced you to think at a systems level. Out of thirteen officers that have had my job over the last forty years, a disproportionate number were CEs. CEs turn up in interesting places; Jack Welch was a CE.

I like to use soap as a metaphor: it's a fundamental truth of chemistry that "like dissolves like." Water alone takes sugar off your hands, but will not take grease off. That requires an organic (carbon)-based substance. Soap is unique in that it is both organic and inorganic; its molecules are attracted to both. Leadership needs to be like that. CEs are systems thinkers; part of that is the ability to make binary couples, so there are always at least a couple of views incorporated in everything they do. This can certainly be developed. Everyone has some leadership skill, and everyone's skill can be improved. And folks do come with different valences.

Leadership is about viewing the world as systems; leaders are people who are stewards of the whole, rather than owners of the parts.

LM: What was your first experience of, or discovery of, your ability to lead?

JD: Before I answer that question, the first leader I ever *noticed* was Lucille Boyden, the promotions director at a resort I worked at in the Smoky Mountains. She was formerly director of the Duke Endowment. This was the mid-sixties, I was sixteen or seventeen, and she let me see "This is the way it is, this is the way it needs to be and let's get it over here. Where should it go and how might we organize to get it there?" Seeing that, seeing someone think that way, was very powerful for me. The earlier you're exposed to that and how excited you are by it may say something about how far you'll go as a leader.

In my own experience: it started in sports, in high school. Growing up in a remote area, I was sent to boarding school in Knoxville — that was the place I first had followers. That's where I learned that it really does help to be brighter. If you can make the pieces come together, it offers a forum for leadership. I should say that Edward deBono's work on teams, however points out that intelligence is not the strongest correlation of leadership — at least not I.Q.; maybe E.Q., emotional intelligence.

LM: How have your gifts matured over time?

JD: How that gift has changed is primarily through pure training. My colleague Pam O'Dell talks about how "Money is the hydraulic fuel of our business; if you understand how the money flows, you understand how the business works." I took a master's degree in finance and the mysteries of the world were revealed.

I also developed, through time, the concept of technical conscience; for this, I owe one of the foundation thinkers of modern naval aviation, Dr. Al Somoroff.

I jealously guard my credibility at the personal level. The techniques of handling thirty, 300 or 30,000 people at NAVAIR don't change, they just scale. I am trying to work harder at celebrating successes. That's hard for systems thinkers, because there's always so much that isn't right.

LM: When do you know you've received the call to leadership?

JD: Is it a calling or is it a motive force looking for a fit? For my (Myers-Briggs) type, it might well be the latter. Running around on the Internet is a matrix of short definitions for the various Myers-Briggs Type Indicator categories. My category, ENTJ (Extroverted, iNtuitive, Thinking, Judging) has the following short definition: "The rest of you will be okay once I get you organized."

LM: When do you recognize it in someone else? How?

JD: The answer to this question is multi-disciplinary, and different mixes can yield that amalgam that you and I would recognize as leadership. It is a collection, not a recipe. Our Naval test pilots get a million-dollar education; 1/3 of it is technical, 1/3 of it is flying and 1/3 of it is communication skills.

I'm good at finding leaders. I look for a "here's a way forward" attitude, systems thinking and tolerance for ambiguity. There are different facets. Emotional I.Q. is not quick; it's not love at first sight. It is an observation over time of stimulus and response, success criteria. "How will we know if we succeed?" Only someone with a desire to lead would ask that. They also have a sense of engagement: "I'm here; I have to engage, not just occupy space." Leaders collect experiences, leaders collect stories.

One observation I've made is that a key trait of a good test pilot is that on the morning of a flight they have the confidence of having done it before. That's because they rehearsed the flight last night in their minds, experienced it virtually. I think it describes good leaders as well: leaders have already played it through in their minds before. As a result, it's much harder to blindside them. They have a kind of unique tactile memory: their body remembers effective responses even when their head doesn't.

LM: How do you know the call has been answered?

JD: I know the call's been answered when I see objectives, success criteria, feedback loops. I have a particular bias: I went through the first half of my leadership life believing that *any* criticism was destructive. Being "tolerant of genius" was my goal. I thought that we risked too much when we shut gifted people down or tried to fit them in boxes. Now I have learned that "if it's not working, change it." So I'm more willing to ask a "genius" to alter his or her behavior if it's a problem for other people.

It's a damn wonder we ever graduate any military leaders; we ask them to do well at every job we give them. Nobody's good at *everything*. It's so competitive at every level; how can you run the system that way and not suppress genius? Obviously, I'm a maverick in this system.

LM: What do you as a leader need from others in order to be effective? What roles do you need them to play?

JD: I need completer-organizers. I need stimulating people, and what I call "quantoids," or number crunchers. I don't make decisions at the first order quantitatively, but I need those facts, those details.

I'm accused of having an inner circle. And it's true. But what people fail to understand is there's no barrier to entry — you just have to be courageous, outspoken, willing to contribute, an idea generator and a systems thinker. Then you can walk in.

LM: Describe your own leadership journey.

JD: That connection between what is and what should be that I first observed or experienced working for Lucille Boyden — I kind of liked it. My mom was a manager in the recreation department of that resort, so I went to work there at fourteen. I got to watch her lead. Then I took officers' training for the Navy in my last two summers in college. I think that officers' training is wonderful for leaders, regardless of whether you stay in. The military spends a lot of time thinking about and promoting leadership and exposes a broad section of the population to that thinking.

My first real leadership challenge came after college. As a CE student, I was a part-time analytical chemist at an EPA lab in Triangle Park, North Carolina, which actually meant I washed bottles. Then, after I graduated, I went from bottle-washer to boss in a week. Doing that, I saw the social aspects of leadership, the role of pride in leadership and followership, how egos interplay, how your tactics have to change depending on how you arrived.

Fortunately, I had friends and I got mentoring from a "gray-beard." I took the position that "I work for all of you; you don't work for me." I did all right. Then I went to flight school, and since then I've had wonderful opportunities to work for great leaders and a few not so great.

I've learned to watch and to garner good tools and good skills. That probably came from watching Lucille: I became an eclectic collector of tools that work. I've noticed that few things succeed like success; you have to have some successes along your way to leadership maturity. As a senior leader, you have to make sure your junior folks have some successes, too.

LM: What do you think is its destination?

JD: By definition, there is no destination to your leadership journey; it is a journey, not a destination. It's more fun to contemplate the trip and set out than to arrive. There's no "place to reach" on a leadership *journey*; only the young and the foolish think they do it well. I think there's some distribution on a continuum of leadership. On the right side are the folks who are driven to lead; they cannot fail to do so. On the other side, we see people motivated to lead out of a sense of service, not intrinsically "called" to lead; they're there out of responsibility, not desire.

LM: What gets in the way of your leadership?

JD: Opportunities. Some of them self-generated, some externally imposed. Too much you want to do. You use up your personal duty cycle and the duty cycle of your staff. My wife gave me the daily reader for *Men Who Try to Do Too Much* — of course I read it all immediately! Part of my maturity has been to discipline that. I've learned to pick some boutique projects that have potential, use them to grow folks and save some time for them.

I hate cookbook leaders. "We're going to do what I read about last week for the next six months." That just tells me they have no sense of self, no proven ethos. I'm also suspicious of a research protocol that doesn't incorporate failure. When you make organizational success the discriminator for leadership success, I worry that you miss something. You lose the ones who took a hopeless company and made it average, or who provided great leadership but in the wrong context (time or place). An absolute measure of leadership may have been "How far did you move it?," not just "Was is a success by today's definition?"

LM: What are the dilemmas that cause you the greatest concern?

JD: For me, one dilemma is trying to find the right balance between genius and social acceptability. I have a guy who eighty percent of the leadership team would define as a problem: giant ego, questionable people skills and a technical genius. I think it's really about asking the question "Do you want a thousand well-behaved, mediocre painters or a shot at a masterpiece?" If you want the masterpiece, then you have to be prepared for someone who's going to cut his ear off. It's the responsibility of senior leadership to fly top cover for those people.

In the military, we promote relatively slowly. People typically spend a considerable, if not set, time at each grade on the way up. It is a purposeful attempt to say to the broad population, "You and all your peers have a long opportunity to reach the top." When you fast-track someone, the message is they've been selected to succeed and thus, implicitly, the rest of you have been selected for something else — failure.

LM: What have been your most transformational experiences as a leader?

JD: I call them inflection points. One was my first really big job, that moment when you realize that up until this point, you have succeeded with personal skill and the interface of a relatively small group. To go from that to realizing "this is going to take thousands of folks," that's a scary moment. Will your skill set scale up to being able to take this quantum leap in terms of leadership challenge?

Another, more personal one was over twenty years ago, when I had a fairly dramatic aircraft crash. We probably should have jumped instead of trying to land. So I've had the experience of listening to steel break up around my body and thinking, "Well, I suspect this is it." I came out of that experience unhurt, and greatly appreciating friends, flowers and beauty. It meant I learned to enjoy the freedom to experiment, that this is all extra time. Ever since then I've carried a strong sense that time is a precious commodity and there's so much to do.

LM: What do you understand about leadership now that you didn't five years ago? Ten?

JD: Ten years ago, I was chief test pilot for the Navy. As a result, I was tapped to talk about Tail Hook on network news. That meant I developed a deep recognition of the importance of public opinion, perception, the press and the politics of it all.

I've learned lots of little tricks. I once had two jobs simultaneously at a lab in California: I was military chief of staff and held a line job as well. I got to write myself action memos! I loved it. How do you teach the elephant to dance? How do you get movement started? How do you step out of the paralysis of analysis and ambiguity and get started? Leadership has to reach out to both the great people and the not-so-great people and get things to work.

I've been a Flag Officer [an admiral] since 1997. In those five years, I've shifted focus from personal leadership to organizational shaping. I'd seen, in my own past, a failure to institutionalize, a failure to put things in place that could be sustained without personal leadership support. I didn't want to replicate that, so I've tried to take the change agentry stuff and make it last.

LM: How have you evolved or matured?

JD: In terms of evolving, I've learned how to read a book in twenty minutes. What a wonderful gift! It gave me back something I'd lost, the exposure to fresh ideas and literature. I still have a bit of temper, not bad, but I can still get mad, and when you get mad as a three-star admiral, it hurts people. I am acutely aware that a stressed relationship between me and someone else can cause the loss of weeks of productivity. I learned recently — reading Welch's book — to follow up by saying "I only get mad at the strong ones."

LM: When you set out to seriously lead, does it take away from life balance?

JD: I'm reminded of a guy I've worked with who is fond of saying, "I don't want any stinking life balance; I want fanatical dedication!" I don't go that far, but leading large enterprises is a duty cycle issue. It gives back wonderful gifts, comradeship, association and great teams. But don't kid yourself; an easier life is to be found in non-leadership. Leaders are more fulfilled, but the quality of life can be pretty sucky.

MONSTERS

UNTAMED BY WHAT WE NEED
THE NATURE OF MONSTERS AND
HOW WE MEET THEM

Winning does not tempt that man,
Winning does not tempt that woman.
This is how s/he grows:
By being defeated, decisively,
By constantly greater beings.

~ ADAPTED BY DAVID WHYTE FROM RILKE, *The Man Watching*

What gets in the way of our effectively assuming leadership, whether in our own life or in our organizations? What prevents us from seeing our dreams realized, from fully owning our potential for greatness, however that might manifest itself?

The external obstacles are easily identified — limited resources (such as money and time), negative attitudes and/or lack of organizational commitment, unexpected changes in the environment, be they economic, political and/or social, micromanagers and the constant crises that result from a management system geared to fire-fighting. Yet at the root, each of these obstacles simply masks deeper issues. For it is never the crisis or the issue itself that is the obstacle on the path to our success, much as we may seduce ourselves into blaming it.

Ultimately, the real monsters we face on our leadership journey are the ones carried inside, monsters that are illuminated by our responses. Do we declare defeat the first time it is announced there aren't enough resources, or do we decide to get creative? Do we figure out ways to move from reactive to proactive in a system that thrives on setting fires and then putting them out? Do we allow ourselves to be defined and defeated by micromanaging bosses, or accept that taking flak is part of the job if we want to see something bigger accomplished? When we don't get the support we hunger for, do we have strength enough to provide it to the team anyway? Are the changes in the environment really the crisis, or is this crisis our lack of resilience, our unwillingness to learn, our own failure to see the opportunities that also accompany the changes?

The real monsters are almost always internal. At the end of the day, the central point is not what "they" did to us. It is how we prevented/minimized/responded. Such monsters speak to the essence of both who we are and how far we have come on our leadership journey.

One reason cyclist Lance Armstrong has such respect as an athlete is that he openly faced one of the great monsters — cancer — and through his own inner strength, conquered his fears (and the monster) and returned to cycle racing's top slot. His perseverance, openness and (newfound) humility have moved people deeply.

The Monster of Who We Are

There's a line from an old cartoon strip, *Pogo*, that captures the essence of the monster of who we are: "We have met the enemy and they is us." It is intrinsic to human nature that, at their core, people get in their own way far more than anyone else ever can. Some of us recognize this early in life and begin to address it; others spend most of their lives discovering the power of the self-fulfilling prophecy. And, of course, some die blaming others for self-induced misery.

How exactly can we be our own monster? Let's begin by looking again at biology, specifically the neurology of our limbic systems, our mammalian brains. When frightened or threatened, most primates suffer from what Daniel Goleman has labeled an "amygdala hijacking."[102] Simply put, two small glands called "the amygdala," located in the limbic system (the mammalian brain), end-run or overpower the thinking brain (the neo-cortex) because they sense danger. They activate the oldest part of us, the brain stem or reptilian brain, engendering the "fight, flee or freeze" response. (Which response is activated depends both on circumstances and the specifics of our individual neurological wiring.)

While those three choices have undoubtedly served to keep primates alive for hundreds of thousands of years, there is no denying that they instantly bankrupt the leadership role. Blood is rerouted from the brain to the hands if the message is "fight," to the legs if the message is "flee" and to both if it is "freeze." Muscles around the rib cage tighten so that the predator can't hear you breathing. Enormous amounts of adrenaline and cortisol are pumped into one's system. These are the chemicals that support short-term, intensive activity — but can kill if they remain at elevated levels for long periods of time. For some people, the tongue is also paralyzed.[103]

Choice and creativity disappear. With a full-blown amygdala hijacking, there can only be reaction. The leader rushing blindly into battle because he or she has no biological choice can no more provide great leadership than the leader who freezes or flees the field. And in today's work world, where physical action is rarely an appropriate response, leadership under those neurological conditions is even more unlikely. It is the rare person who can maintain and prevent a personal amygdala hijacking in the midst of a group panic attack.

Nigel Morris, founder and CEO of Capital One, the financial services company, in a keynote speech to the National Leadership Institute Conference on Coaching in 1999, credited his personal coach for the increased maturity that enabled him not to lose his head during a week in which the company's stock lost forty percent of its value. Due to his three years of coaching, Morris recognized that, as a leader, he didn't have the luxury of succumbing to terror, but had to hold the boundaries and create the container of assurance within which everyone else could mentally return to work.

The dilemma in this dynamic is that the amygdala is not a very discriminating sorter: *any* element in the current situation that harkens back to *any* element in *any* past situation in which the person experienced threat, humiliation, embarrassment or shame will alert the reptilian brain, home of the fight-flee-or-freeze response. Does a neighbor resemble a bullying classmate from fourth grade? Does a friend's gesture bring back memories of how Dad didn't ever seem to listen? Even triggers as subtle as these will "awaken the reptile." If that past memory relates to something sufficiently traumatic, it can induce a full-blown amygdala hijacking.

This reaction is further complicated by gender differences. Both women and men have fight-or-flight responses to life-threatening situations. Apparently, males tend to have reptilian responses to not only life-threatening, but a wide variety of stressful situations. When not faced with threat or humiliation, however, females' response to stress is significantly different. Labeled "tend and befriend" by scientists, it appears to be an extension of women's affiliative inclinations that cause them, under stress, to be more likely to reach for connection than to pick a fight, freeze or withdraw. [104]

While undoubtedly more adaptive to today's workplaces, tend-and-befriend responses also come at a cost — the person taking on relationship responsibility may not have the resources to sustain it. Male or female, such a reactive response is not inevitable. However, it takes considerable maturity, insight and self-discipline to understand oneself well enough to prevent amygdala hijackings. Not only must a person be able to recognize vulnerabilities and hot-buttons in himself, he must also consciously develop strategies for preventing reptilian responses, both to threat and to stress. For some, the path to such deep self-knowledge and self-control may lie through coaching or some type of personal therapy. For others, practice in the martial arts or meditation may be the way.

Monsters All Around

Beyond the biological, there are a large number of other opportunities to be our own monster, our own worst enemy. In fact, there are monsters to be found in four other domains of life: emotional, intellectual, moral and spiritual. Chief amongst the emotional monsters is **ego**: that driving need to be the one in charge or in control, the one in the spotlight, the one who is right, the one who has all the answers, the one who has the most, the one who does it all. Like Peter Pan, most people want to win every battle and outsmart the enemy every time. And perhaps, for a time, it may actually happen in just that way. Yet no one wins every battle.

When Andy Pearson was CEO of PepsiCo, *Fortune* called him one of the ten toughest bosses in America. Twenty years later, as founding chairman of Tricon Global Restaurants (KFC, Pizza Hut and Taco Bell), Pearson, (now in his seventies, which only proves one is never too old to learn) is acquiring new leadership skills. When Pearson arrived at Tricon's corporate offices for the first time to a band playing and hundreds of employees cheering, he knew he was in a new story: "All the time I was at Pepsi, nothing remotely like this had ever happened. It was overwhelming. I knew something was going on that was fundamentally very powerful. If we could learn how to harness that spirit with something systematic, then we would have something unique."[105]

Over the past few years, Pearson has come to realize that the heart is the key to a company's competitive edge, and that if limbic needs are fundamental to human beings, then working with those needs is not a weakness but a strength. His view of leadership has changed: "Your real job is to get results and to do it in a way that makes your organization a great place to work — a place where people enjoy coming to work, instead of just taking orders and hitting this month's numbers."[106]

For Pearson, that change — his transition through the wormhole — had to do with reining in his ego. "I proved that I was smart by finding fault with other people's ideas. I think I've gone from making my way by trying to be the smartest guy in the room to just asking questions and insisting that the answers be reasonable and logical."[107] His move into elderhood wasn't about not asking those hard questions. It was about no longer asking them to prove how smart he was, but asking them in service of the larger, organizational good. He notes:

> Ultimately, it's all about having more genuine concern for the other person. There's a big difference between being tough and being tough-minded. There's an important aspect that has to do with humility. But I've been modestly disappointed at how hard it is to get leaders to act that way. I think it's going to take a generation of pounding away on this theme. We've got a half-dozen or so real leaders in our company, but we don't have twenty or thirty. You know what it takes? Role models.[108]

That lack of role models is epidemic. It speaks deeply to the stories we carry about leadership today. The transition from a results-driven, no-room-for-feelings business manager to someone who leads from her heart is, again, a story of a wormhole experience — someone who suddenly recognizes an alternative reality and must undergo an intensely personal transformation, facing her monsters, to get there.

Ego can also take the form of a driven narcissism that tells us that we are somehow responsible for *everything*. Or it can show up as temper, an inability to handle things not going our way without anger. But sooner or later, we do not have the right answer, we do not have the capacity to do it all, we cannot win the battle — and we are forced to face our limitations. For most of us, this is experienced as a breakdown, a failure. Yet in that very moment of failure — be it large and dramatic or small and gradual — lies the secret of growth, the wormhole transformation that might catapult us to the next level. Then we can honor our leadership call and move another step toward elderhood.

Similarly (or simultaneously), the monster we do battle with may be one of **insecurities**. We may not see what is evident to everyone else: the gift is there, and others will follow, if we will but ask or act. Indeed, the internal conversation about not being good enough can be so loud that it distracts from data that is immediately at hand, data that says we are on the right track and that others want us to lead. Caught up in our own self-assessments, we spread our anxiety as though it were a virus, and indeed it is — a highly contagious "thought virus" that can quickly infect everyone around us.

This failure to contain anxiety[109] is a significant human experience, one that has special impact when leaders succumb to it. It is one monster that often spawns a host of others, as people begin to doubt everything about their leaders, the organization's direction and the purpose of their work. As General Burgoyne, the famed British general who lost to superior American forces during the Revolutionary War is said to have noted, "When the general panics, so do the troops."

Arrogance is probably the most common intellectual monster in our workplaces. It often manifests itself as a kind of locking into a system of thinking that prevents other possibilities from being recognized until too late. Intellectual investment in a certain way of thinking, a certain way of analyzing the world, lends itself to "ownership of the parts," rather than "stewardship of the whole,"[110] and tends to generate rigidity, making organizations vulnerable to new competitors, new technologies or changes in the markets they serve.

Depression is a spiritual monster that more and more rears its ugly head in the work world. As a May/June, 2003 *Psychology Today* article reports:

One top executive who "met the monster and made it through" contends that being crowned king is itself the problem. "You discover that the real fun was getting there," he says. "Once you're there you live in fear that you're going to lose it. Not only is achieving the goal a letdown, you don't feel good about yourself as a 'master of the universe.' You treat people differently. You believe in your own bullshit." ... At the senior management level, he says, "Depression is rampant among people who have achieved their goals — and even worse among those who have not."[111]

Ultimately, depression is a failure to have found meaning in life. Viewed as emotional, most people feel that speaking about depression is unacceptable in the workplace. They must appear tough, competent and clear-headed at all times. The fear of being "discovered," when the price may be a literal one, as the organization's market value is affected, or less direct, as a plum assignment is directed elsewhere, feeds a vicious cycle of loneliness and despair.

Greed is perhaps the ugliest moral monster, one that often seduces us into self-betrayal, the Faustian bargain that excuses behavior that corrodes from the inside out. It may be greed for money or for power or for the trappings of power. In all cases, the thing a person is greedy for — whether it takes the form of power, perks or dollars — is a sense of self-worth that can't ultimately be filled by such symbolic forms.

Whether it is more stock options, the next degree or that next promotion, sooner or later the sense of accomplishment seems to give way to the greed monster, and the search must begin again. Be it the acquisition of tulips, land, junk bonds or dot-coms, the greed monster is present until — through maturing — one moves beyond it. Greed often requires an especially brutal wake-up call — loss of a loved one, loss of family and friends or even a near-death experience, resulting in the recognition that the hole is not being filled by greater wealth or higher status and never will be — for the greedy person to break free.

The Monster of How Far One Has Come on the Journey

What is the source of all these monsters, from overblown ego to rampaging insecurity? Why do the monsters surface one day and not the next? One day we may be quite capable of simply focusing on what needs to be done and the next day unable to do so.

The source is this: our own growth and development. As humans, we spend our emotional lives caught between twin poles:

* a powerful desire for autonomy, for independence, for self-hood and separation, and
* an equally powerful desire for connection, for community, for affiliation and intimacy.

Within this ambivalence lie the monsters.

"Our experience of this fundamental ambivalence may be our experience of the unitary, restless, creative motion of life itself."[112] In the process of maturing, we spend our lives spiraling upward between these two poles, periodically touching base with each and then pushing off to a higher level that absorbs and integrates everything that has come before. For some, it is a path punctuated by wormhole experiences; for others it is more gradual. Either way, this movement between two poles is the deep structure of the leadership journey.

If a person stops maturing, he stays stuck, clinging to one pole or another, unable to let go of his current commitments to autonomy ("I don't need anyone else, I can do this by myself!") or connection ("I need someone else, I can't do anything by myself.") But the pull to move on will never really go away, and much of that person's available energy may be sapped in resisting it.

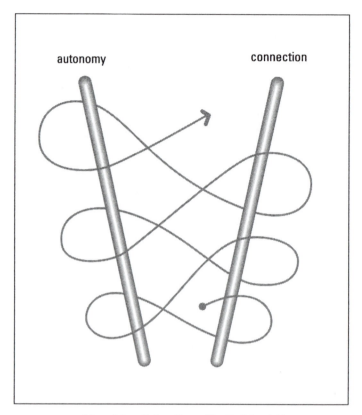

Adapted from Robert Kegan, The Evolving Self

Some of the effectiveness of a leader clearly depends on the fit between where she finds herself on that evolving continuum and the demands of the moment. If that person finds herself, her core identity, resting comfortably at one of the poles, she experiences a clear basis for action and movement from that place. It doesn't matter if it is the pole of the independent, autonomous self or that of the connected, communal self. For the moment, she "knows" herself, and the internal chatter is stilled: it is easy to attend effectively to the external world, and she experiences life as deeply centered and focused.

When a person is truly on the leadership journey, he awakens one morning to find himself moved by life off the pole, drawn inexorably to the next stage in his own development, and then suddenly he has a very different experience. His old stories about his "self," about who and how he is no longer work. He has not yet evolved new stories to replace them.

"I'm just not myself," is a phrase that, invariably tells me, as a coach, that life has bumped this person off a position on one of the poles. Thrown unwillingly into transition, (specifically Bridges' "neutral zone," referred to earlier, where all things are possible and nothing predictable,[113]) most of us panic, at least until we better understand what is happening and why. Panicked and grieving at the loss of the old self, we often return to the dynamics of the reptilian brain described earlier in this chapter.

Facing Essential Pain

Robert Kegan, in his powerful integration of human development theory, *The Evolving Self*, notes that growth involves

> ...more than a new relationship between self and other; it involves a new *construction* of self and others; it involves a redrawing of the line where I stop and you begin, a redrawing that eventually consists in a qualitatively new guarantee to you of your distinctness from me (permitting at the same time a qualitatively "larger" you with which to be in relation).[114]

This construction of a new and larger self occurs over and over, whether we are moving from the autonomy pole, convinced of our independent capabilities and fundamental aloneness, or from the connection pole, deeply committed to relationship and community. Each time it involves a powerful (and often terrifying) period of "not knowing" — not knowing where the boundaries are, not knowing what is ours and what belongs to others. We must ask ourselves: what can be brought out from the old self to help constitute the new self? What must now be left behind?

We are all familiar with the childhood cycles of this experience, whether it is the "terrible twos" (who Kegan suggests are not loudly saying "no!" to the external world, but "no" to the self they are leaving behind[115]) or the more complex and painful push-pulls between independence and connection that characterize the adolescent's path. As Kegan notes,

> ... these self-other distinctions are in fact, tenuous, fragile, precarious states. They are balances, I have said: they can tip over. They are truces, I have said: chaos and a state of siege lie around the corner.[116]

While this description captures the adolescent experience, it equally well describes an adult leader who is being called to the next level of leadership development.

The young leader, receiving criticism from his manager, finds himself suddenly unable to discern the boundaries between himself and his work or what he truly knows to be right, let alone the meaning of the apparent loss of approval from such a significant "other." He loses the way to make meaning in the current situation, and the balance tips into chaos.

Even a mature leader, faced with a crisis, can quickly find herself deeply thrown into a state of siege, losing sight of the fact that what happens to her is not the same as what happens to her organization. Pulled from the pole on which he or she had been resting comfortably, each must now experience the profoundly frightening discomfort of learning a new way to be, a higher way to function in the world. This is the essential pain of leadership growth.

For others, or at other times on the journey, the next step on the journey may be internally generated; there is a dissatisfaction with current life, a sense of suffocation, alienation or despair that reflects a call to "function at a higher or deeper level, to find a way to live that has more significance and depth, to find out who you are beyond the social persona that you and your environment have jointly created."[117] As Carol Pearson puts it,

> When we do so, our seeking takes on a different, deeper quality. Suddenly, we are seeking spiritual depth and authenticity, and we know it is not just a change in environment — mates, work, place — we seek, but a change in ourselves.[118]

It has again become time to let go of the pole on which we have been resting and move on. Again we must face the essential human terror of not knowing, having to relearn both the world and ourselves.

Performer or Learner: How Will You Face the Journey?

Research on children's approaches to learning by Carol Dweck, a professor of psychology at Columbia University, holds an important key to the roots of one's motivation for that learning as adults.[119] It speaks deeply, in turn, to how people handle themselves in transition on their leadership journey.

Dweck observed that children who believed their performance was a measure of their ability became quickly discouraged when they ran into difficulties. Such "performer" children assumed that experiencing difficulty indicated an innate lack of ability, because ability was, by definition, fixed and permanent. On the other hand, children who did not assume that ability was fixed were stimulated or challenged by difficulties and threw themselves into resolving them. Experimenting with both greater effort and different strategies, they saw (and experienced) their effort as the road to increased capability.

Performers focus on doing things well and avoiding failure. In order to avoid the risk of a less-than-perfect performance, they avoid activities where practice and the risk of making mistakes will be necessary to develop mastery. Instead, performers stick to what already comes easily (their natural abilities), thereby inhibiting the development of new capabilities. As a result, they don't commit to endeavors that might require a higher level of performance than they believe themselves capable of offering.

Learners focus differently. They are driven far more by curiosity than by concern with how others perceive their performance. Their concern thus is with action ("What happens if I try this?") rather than with how their results are judged. Mistakes become simple feedback, rather than symbols of failure. They adjust and try again to reach their goals. Learners tolerate a lot of frustration and mistakes on the road to accomplishing what they want. They do not judge themselves as failures for not getting it right the first, the second or even the third time. As a result, their capabilities continue to expand.

Recent research by Edward Hirt at Indiana University Bloomington adds a possible gender component to the performer-learner dynamic. Using a neutrally named subject, 888 people were asked to react to the subject's electing to go to the movies rather than study for a big exam. Whether the subject was viewed as male or female did not influence participant's assessments, but Hirt notes:

> Guys seem to value competence to a greater extent. They don't really see effort as inherently good by itself. ...Women have very strong belief systems about effort withdrawal. They pride themselves on being hard workers.[120]

This may help to explain some of the difficulties women leaders — who often adopt a story of overcoming obstacles through hard work in order to succeed — occasionally face. If their male colleagues don't value that story, and only want to see quickly demonstrated competence, such women can be at a disadvantage.

In reality, like the rest of us, most leaders function as performers in some arenas and learners in others. The dilemma is that, if at moments of transition in a person's life, we revert to performer mode, our focus is on how we are perceived by others. We lose the opportunity to listen to and discover our new and evolving self, the opportunity to mature. We may even lose the possibility of discovering the leader emergent within. We are, in essence, refusing the call to elderhood.

If, on the other hand, we can face such transitions as a seeker, as a learner, if we can access our hunger to "participate in the grandeur of the universe — whether it is through a great love, a great work, the ultimate experience, personal transformation or the attainment of wisdom,"[121] then the moments of transition are more easily accepted as part of the process. Even if such moments throw us back to the monsters, they can also strengthen our conviction that there is always more to be learned. When we are fascinated by what we are learning, the discomfort — even the terror — fades, and we can move more easily and gracefully through that which earlier would have been only suffering and loss.

The great contribution of Dweck's research came later in her career, when she began to see that language had an enormous impact on the performer/learner dynamic. Having assumed that the preferences for learner or performer were innate, she was startled to discover that performer children could turn into learners by the way feedback was given.

Feedback that focused solely on results created performers. Feedback that focused on the process — how hard they worked, how creative or imaginative or persistent they were — created learners. In other words, feedback that focuses on the fruits of curiosity and actions turns people into learners. Feedback that focuses solely on results creates performers.

This at least partially answers the question about whether leadership is innate or can be taught, as well as addressing the questions about whether there are clear ways to grow and develop leaders. Certainly leadership can be "untaught" through the ways in which organizations reward and recognize leadership behavior. If only short-term results matter, bullies can be perceived as leaders. (Such reward systems also fuel the greed monster.)

If curiosity, innovation and generativity matter, then we get a deeper, richer version of leadership. Thus, we can teach leadership when we encourage and reward learning and growth. Surely much of the current ill health of corporate, non-profit and political leadership can be traced to this dynamic. We've become so focused on short-term performance that we inexorably press our leadership into being performers and squeeze the learner out of them. In this way, Wall Street is its own monster, as the junk bonds of the eighties and the dot-coms of the nineties so vividly illustrated.

Conclusion: Meeting the Enemy

In Campbell's architecture of the great stories, the heroes inevitably must confront monsters, and, in so doing, they are forced to greater levels both of competence and self-awareness. In Beowulf's story, when the hero slays Grendel, he awakens and must then fight Grendel's mother, a far more fearsome monster.

So, too, when we face the easy monsters as Peter Pan leaders, we awaken larger forces that cannot be denied if we are to grow into mature leaders. We must confront our biological and emotional weaknesses and our yearnings for greatness, to be part of something larger than ourselves. Those weaknesses and yearnings are the true monsters. We must face and resolve the issues they represent if our hero's journey is to unfold and the story come to fruition.

ON THE PATH OF LIGHT
AND SHADOW
JULIO OLALLA OF
THE NEWFIELD NETWORK

Julio Olalla is the founder of the Newfield Network. Newfield is an international education and consulting organization with headquarters in Chile and North America. Newfield believes it is not possible to face the profound and constant changes of the world effectively without a serious effort toward organizational and personal transformation. Julio has trained over 50,000 individuals in advanced communication skills, coaching and leadership throughout North and South America, Europe and Australia. Julio is also a powerful keynote speaker, having addressed large audiences in England, Argentina, Canada, Switzerland and the U.S. His message inspires audiences to review not only the content of what they are thinking and learning, but also their interpretation of learning itself.

Julio has an enormous gift as a coach for helping people face their monsters, possibly because he has had to face such big ones himself— the military overthrow of a democratically-elected government in his native Chile, exile, etc. I put this conversation here because, in my experience of him, Julio consistently uses love to face the monsters, without ever compromising integrity, dignity or accountability and without resorting to oversimplification. His own journey is one that has carried him into ever larger realms and provides a great illustration of the Third Principle story. I'm also struck by how the spiritual domain has expanded for him. If Julio's syntax seems unique, it's because English is not his first language.

LISA MARSHALL: Julio, you and I both know that the conversation we have today about leadership is, as David Whyte says, "not commensurate with the world we are entering." We don't seem to have ways to talk about what we're asking of our leaders — and ourselves. I'm specifically concerned that we have no concept of leadership maturity, no live conversation about what that might be or how it might be achieved. Tell me your thoughts on maturity, please.

JULIO OLALLA: A way I have talked about maturity or adulthood has to do with capacity to take responsibility in all domains of life. That's different than doing all things. You can delegate some things, but not everything. For example, you can't delegate paternity, but you can delegate administration (remembering that delegating doesn't mean you aren't still responsible.) When we are teenagers, we haven't yet assumed responsibility for all domains of our life. Aiming to take responsibility, instead of being into claiming innocence, that is adulthood.

Adulthood is an absent conversation culturally. We aren't even aware of the transition. And we mostly don't believe it: "I'm not really an adult!" Sometimes even today I don't believe it. We don't have the rituals that announce adulthood. We don't have a way to recognize that we have taken ownership of responsibility in every domain of living.

Human beings live with a huge longing, a longing to be one; it is the core mystical longing. In maturity, we hit transcendence for the first time. We arrive to a point where what is beyond us becomes relevant to us. The inability to be in touch with transcendence is immaturity.

LM: What's your definition of leadership?

JO: First of all, when we say that someone is a leader, we are making an assessment. It could happen that a person is a leader in the eyes of someone but not in the eyes of someone else. So, we must ask some questions: when we call somebody a leader, what are we assessing? What actions or ways of being are we noticing in someone to call her a leader? What is common in the actions or ways of being of people who are assessed as leaders?

In which ways can a human being provide meaning, inspiration, guidance and direction to other human beings? I believe that it is through a narrative, a great story, that is not always explicit, but is often implicit in the actions of the one we call leader. And that great story has the power to provide a role in it to every follower. Whatever the follower does is now full of meaning, it is part of this scenario.

A second aspect of leadership comes from a different set of questions: where is anyone coming from when his actions move others to call him a leader? What common forces are at work in those people we assess as leaders? What fire are they burning in? What cosmic force makes them storytellers and key players in that story? These two aspects of leadership must be considered to understand the phenomenon. They are necessary elements of a good definition of leadership, a definition that I don't have yet.

I want to add something here: we have said that leaders generate seductive narratives, what I've called great stories. Those stories generate meaning to the followers, give them a great scheme within which they place their own actions. But here we need to be careful. Meaning does not come simply out of a story, understood as a conceptual construction. Meaning comes from the emotional make-up of the story, the mood that the story elicits. This is a critical aspect of leadership. Leaders create the right emotional context for the task to be performed.

LM: What is the source of the drive to do that? What is that cosmic force you describe?

JO: I've come to believe that the great process of our lives is the desire of the universe to know itself. The cosmos wants to know itself. We are one sparkle within a greater consciousness. My knowing does not belong to me; it's in service of that greater task. This process takes place in multiple forms: cultivating the land, manufacturing, discussing different perspectives, through analysis, intuitively, poetically, mystically, empirically, through different forms of art, religiously, analogically, etc. Reducing this phenomenon to a "self" misses its greatness. It's a collective process; therefore, leadership is constitutive of it.

Galileo lived a great dilemma: to be faithful to his truth and good to the people he loved. Or to put it differently, listening to two forces: what wanted to manifest and what was threatened to be left behind. He lived a huge pressure. That's what happens to us individually in our own processes of learning, that's what happens to us culturally, that's what happens universally. That enormous pressure, very often manifested as suffering, is the generative mechanism of new thoughts, new practices, new insights and new understandings of reality. Those two forces shape leaders as much as those leaders allow those forces to take shape.

LM: What was your first experience of, or discovery of, your ability to lead?

JO: I was a high school student and I was elected "president" of my class. I think I was thirteen years old. There was something about me that was puzzling to my peers: I was able to engage in serious conversations. And the subjects we addressed were unusual: life, suffering, joy, the world. All of that really meant a lot to me. At that time my parents had just divorced, I was very sad and my sadness legitimized the sadness of many others. They dared to speak what had been unspeakable so far. That's the first time I felt I was leading.

Why do some of the things I do deserve the assessment of leadership? Maybe it is my storytelling, the relationship that is created in the storytelling — the emotion of meaningfulness — looking at the place where you have always been and seeing it as if for the first time.

LM: How have your gifts matured over time?

JO: I find myself more at ease, trusting that what I need is available to me and also trusting that I'll be able to listen to what's essential to others. I won't be distracted in the many little stories they may tell, but I'll be able to listen through them to what matters the most, what they are longing for, so I'll be guided.

When I work, I have a sense that something wants to unfold and uses whatever it has at hand to do so. I happen to be well trained to be used to facilitate that. Learning takes place and I don't have to teach.

LM: When do you know you've received the call to leadership?

JO: A story my father told about me is that when I was little, about two and a half, I was found leaning over the fence of the property we lived in, listening in complete fascination to a street preacher with his Bible tucked up under his arm. Later, my father found me standing on a wooden box in the living room, with a book tucked up under my arm, preaching... That's a story I've been told; I don't actually remember it. But when I heard it, it meant a lot to me. It was the call and I can't tell you why.

I was a leader in my high school and later in my professional guild. There was always something in me about serving others and serving something bigger than me.

The force of the call is very distinctive. I feel it very concretely. I feel it in my belly, something heavy in my chest. For a moment it's a burning sensation, then it is a tingling thing, a lot of pleasure. Sometimes when I read I experience the same sensations: the writer is giving voice to something I knew and didn't have words for. A great conversation is the same — a fusing, and a melting.

LM: When do you recognize it in someone else? How?

JO: When we get in touch with the call, we first enter into a turmoil, an intense period of self-doubts and monsters until finally, after a deep process, we illuminate. I'll recognize someone being called when I see him or her daring to face these monsters, willing to go into transformational learning (as opposed to informational learning) as well as when someone creates in me ambitious peace, what you, Lisa, have called "presence."

LM: How do you know the call has been answered?

JO: As I said before: when someone enters into a process of transformational learning. It's not just an issue of being better educated, it's dealing with a serious self-assessment of being insufficient to this large, marvelous, great challenge. Life is seeing from gratitude, and therefore with a great desire to contribute. A courage that we never had before allows us to face all our monsters, our pettiness, and to offer life a greater gift.

We are always called. We listen to the call or we don't. You will find some grayish-ness around those who chose not to answer. The brightness around them has disappeared.

LM: What do you as a leader need from others in order to be effective? What roles do you need them to play?

JO: I need from others to let me serve them. The greater your desire to learn, the greater the teacher I am. I need to be granted the opportunity to be listened to. I need at least a small window of trust. I need their passion as my guiding light.

For the few that are very close to me, I need them to hold me dearly. At the same time as I appear strong, willful, inspired, I know that there is another side of me that is weak, unwilling, uninspired. It is only through the recognition of my shadows that my light comes out. I need those close to me to love me including my shadows, not just as though I am only light.

LM: Describe for me your own leadership journey.

JO: My journey is not extraordinary. I've been pushed by currents and happen to be swimming relatively well. There was no plan, no advance planning — it was survival. I was in exile, deprived of a land, deprived of a language, deprived of a coherent discourse. It was horrendous and, at the same time, the best gift life could have given me. I didn't choose it. It happened to me, and I was lucky enough to connect with some people who helped me to listen to the call and ignited in me a fire that didn't get put out.

A good part of my journey has been a profound desire to serve, to be of use; that's what weaves all the disparate parts together. It didn't start with a sense of direction; it has evolved into a sense of direction. We do a disservice to leaders when we think of them as having an overwhelming sense of clarity.

We have to find narratives that will stick to us emotionally, in order to let go of the ones we're trapped in. Leaders provide that for people. We hold ourselves as the authors of every step, but really we only author it after the step has been taken, not in advance.

LM: What do you think is its destination?

JO: Sometimes I know there is a destination but only sometimes. Once I was an atheist, today I am in a different place. So, yes, there is a destination and our job is to find the road to get there.

LM: What gets in the way of your leadership?

JO: Sometimes it is very hard to give myself credit. Sometimes I confuse "to be humble" with "lacking ownership." That has been in the way. Sometimes, flatly, my history. Being from the Southern Hemisphere, a small corner of the world, it's hard to think large of oneself. I'm not from the parts of the world where history is written. We don't have available to us greatness in the way you do in other parts of the world. If, like Prometheus, I could take the fire of greatness to our land, it would be the belief that we *can* be great.

LM: What are the dilemmas that cause you the greatest concern?

JO: Not to be up to the task is my biggest dilemma. Not to be up to the task, not to have the strength to go all the way, whatever that means. And I have a huge fear to disappoint. That somehow I've opened a big door and maybe there is nothing in there.

LM: What have been your most transformational experiences as a leader?

JO: As a general idea, every occasion in which life shows me, with no mercy, that my interpretations were insufficient. The first time, I was twenty-eight and it was the overthrow of Allende and my country's government. September 11, 2001 was twenty-eight years later to the day.

One huge experience was coming to live in the U.S. It was at the end of the Cold War, and we got to reinvent the game. We're in the middle of that right now, it's a very fruitful place to be, the old labels are gone.

Meeting certain people has been transformational, and I can think of three to four transformational conversations, when I "lost my innocence." For me, it's been through flesh and bones and through wonderful books.

LM: What do you understand about leadership now that you didn't five or ten years ago?

JO: I understand that leadership is not a psychological attribute; it's an expression of an enormously bigger game, a cosmic game in play. And when we talk about leadership, it's a judgment. We are only leaders to those who assess us as leaders for themselves.

LM: How have you evolved or matured?

JO: I put less attention on me. That interpretation I spoke of earlier that I'm the servant of something, the higher point where lightning strikes. At the same time, I'm taking a higher responsibility for my work. I'm open like I never was before to different views, to criticism.

LM: How haven't you evolved or matured?

JO: I became a father at fifty-four, for the third time. I've been reflecting on the Universe, love, what is a good life. Everything has been questioned. The biggest step is to embody my own wisdom, to embrace it. I will never do it completely. There is a larger way of being, which I see, but don't know if I have enough life to learn to be that. At the same time, I am more and more accepting of that — that's the way it is.

LM: What else should we have discussed about leadership?

JO: "Leaders" lead in particular domains. One of the most brutal pressures on leaders is the assumption that they are to lead everywhere, that they are only light or shadows. Remember, the greater the light the sharper the shadows.

In our time, the biggest growth in the capacity of a leader is the ability to be certain without having to resort to the truth. The great leaders go to mystery for certainty, not truth. They give permission to mystery, to wonder, to not knowing, and they become humble servants. We are about to have this, even in business, where you can't possibly handle all the information anymore. The art of judging is closer to the art of leading than the art of being informed.

When people look to me for advice, I go to the mystery, the ambiguity, the paradox, but they find in me certainty. Certainty is an assessment, in the past, we have lived it that we "have the truth," but now it is the certainty of having a path. Leaders create certainty by putting us on a path, not resorting to truth.

Mandela, for me, personifies everything that creates a leader. Simplicity, fierce commitment, humble self-assessment and complete inability to compromise the path he was setting. He embraces the celebration of life; he breathes life in every part of his body. He can speak to anyone because he's not threatened. He has no time for resentment. His job is so large and so meaningful that it's a pity to even think of resenting. I am so grateful to live in his time.

VIII FEELING THE TIDE RISE
FACING OUR MONSTERS

> *Few things are more dangerous than*
> *a leader with an unexamined life.*
>
> ~ JOHN C. MAXWELL

If it is our own demons that need to be faced, our own monsters conquered in each of the four key domains mentioned earlier — emotional, intellectual, spiritual and moral — as much or more than any external challenges, how is that accomplished? Here each leadership journey is as unique as the individual who takes it. For some, intellectual challenges must be overcome. For others, the challenges may be spiritual. For still others, the monsters may be difficult, emotional, moral dilemmas. In any given leader's lifetime, there will be monsters in each of those domains, some easily recognized and dealt with, some deeply buried. While the boundaries between them are sometimes indistinct, what is certain is that greatness in leadership requires maturity — and the willingness to face our monsters — in all domains.

Within each domain, there are elements of maturity which help define potential monsters. With **intellectual** maturity comes a willingness to face reality, to analyze incisively and perform independent and creative thinking, as well as the capacity to see patterns and weave parts into a whole, to see systems and accept a stewardship role for those systems. **Emotional** maturity brings with it a capacity for independence, the willingness to take action as a free agent, along with the capacity to affiliate, to freely initiate and sustain loving relationships. Those with **moral** maturity have the ability to hold fast to their moral compass when others do not, and to stay in dialogue with those whose moral values are different. When we achieve **spiritual** maturity, we develop and maintain spiritual disciplines that allow us to discern where the spirit leads us, along with the capacity to stay connected to that source as well as utilize and return the gifts that life has offered. We shall explore each in detail.

MATURITY DOMAINS

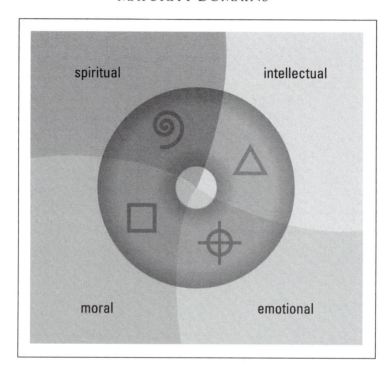

The Meaning of Maturity

Ultimately, maturity is one of those words that, for most of us, falls into the category of "I know it when I see it." The dictionary defines maturity as "fully developed in body or mind, as a person." But what does "fully developed" actually mean?

Maturity is the place where the twin poles of development, our need for autonomy and our need for connection, fully experienced, finally converge. Our struggle shifts in a way that allows us to embrace the space between those poles instead of fearing or resisting it. As mature people, we no longer feel only our true selves when resting comfortably on a developmental pole. We come to understand, consciously or unconsciously, that the space between the poles represents possibility; then we open into it.

The poles are thus bound together in inescapable relationship. When we find our balance in that space of possibility that lives between them, we can truly make meaning of our lives. No longer do we claim innocence: we "step up to the responsibility"[122] of meaning-making in all domains of our lives. We accept that our intellectual, emotional, moral and spiritual choices — and their consequences — are our own.

What is the nature of maturity in each domain? Clearly, the domains intertwine, and the boundaries are soft. Nonetheless, there is value in exploring each domain. To illustrate them, we will refer to five simple shapes that, according to Angeles Arien in *Signs of Life*, carry nearly universal meaning — the circle, the cross, the triangle, the square and the spiral.

Intellectual Maturity

The intellectual domain in leadership may seem cut and dried: leaders are smarter; they know more than the rest of us. The reality is more complex. Leaders do have access to more information than the rest of us, and that information can make a difference. However, years of research by the Center for Creative Leadership, Daniel Goleman and many others have illuminated one of the great paradoxes of leadership — that the gifts that bring you into leadership do not keep you there.

Studies of successful executives and those who derailed show that:

> The managers who failed were almost always high in expertise and IQ. In every case their fatal weakness was in emotional intelligence — arrogance, over-reliance on

brainpower, inability to adapt to the occasionally disorienting economic shifts in that region and disdain for collaboration or teamwork.[123]

It is not surprising that cerebral intelligence — an ability to quickly pick up, manipulate, analyze and regurgitate large amounts of information — gets equated with success in our speed- and performance-driven world. For much of our working lives, it is what is rewarded, and often passes for judgment.

It is also not surprising that we mistake information for knowledge and knowledge for wisdom. Wisdom, the stuff of mature judgment, exists, however, in all four domains: it is possible to be intellectually wise, morally wise, emotionally wise and/or spiritually wise. What, then, does intellectual maturity actually look, sound and feel like?

For leaders, intellectual maturity, in fact, takes them in a very interesting direction. It has as much to do with the size of notions grasped, as the effectiveness with which they are applied. The concept of intellectual maturity moves us along a continuum from concrete to abstract, from finite to infinite. When we shift from "ownership of the parts"[124] (concrete, finite) to "stewardship for the whole,"[125] we have reached intellectual maturity.

The maturity path in this domain includes, as it does in each domain, autonomy and connection. On the autonomy side, intellectual maturity is the willingness to squarely face reality, as well as the capacity to comprehend the multiple, complex systems or patterns in which life, work and spirit flourish. Many corporations move people through a variety of parts of the organization — marketing, engineering, finance, etc., in order to foster such maturity. At another level, the work done in chaos and complexity theory in recent years, addressing aspects of life that science had previously ignored, represents increased intellectual maturity within the scientific community.

Ultimate intellectual maturity may be defined as having the capacity to see through patterns to the underlying wholeness, what physicist David Bohm called "the implicate order." Intellectual maturity discerns that a few simple rules will generate all the complex behavior we need. (Nordstrom's one-page rulebook for employees is a well-known example.) This is where mature judgment is in evidence.

At the same time intellectual maturity holds its constructs lightly and with curiosity, knowing that there are always more questions than answers. Autonomy and connection merge, and when they do, important new spaces open. As an example, David Bohm's work in physics with its emphasis on independent thinking led him to write about dialogue, which is fundamentally a process of creating connection. His unique approach has influenced many who never would have explored his work in physics.

Each domain has monsters clearly unique to it, and many of those monsters overlap. Intellectual monsters can include our being so caught up in the cleverness of our own thinking we fail to listen to others, and perseveration — becoming so caught in a system of thought that we repeat the same loops endlessly. Other monsters include those mentioned earlier: rigidity and a tendency to look only at the parts, not the whole, to analyze the bits and bites without ever seeing the big picture.

The symbol used as the icon for intellectual maturity is the triangle, or arrowhead. It implies a goal, a target, having an end point for our hopes and aspirations. It also represents the power of having clear and compelling outcomes that keep our hopes focused.

INTELLECTUAL MATURITY

Autonomy : willingness to face reality, capacity for incisive analysis and independent creative thinking.

Connection : capacity to see patterns and weave parts into whole, see systems, see stewardship role.

Monsters : cleverness, perseveration, rigidity, ownership of the parts.

Emotional Maturity

Emotional maturity is the form of maturity most widely researched and discussed, both in personal development and in leadership. Because it focuses on the capacity for love, it holds special significance in the conversation about leadership maturity. Yet the boundaries between emotional maturity and other forms of maturity are sometimes elusive. For our purposes, emotional maturity includes all aspects of kinesthetic experience — both tactile sensation, including the felt body or somatic self, and emotional sensation, or the feeling self. It is the domain of relationships, the relationship to oneself and the relationship to others.

Emotional maturity has a clear physical component. Emotionally mature leaders inhabit their bodies fully as well as their brains. They use the sensory data their bodies provide to assess situations and make decisions. This embodied quality enables them to move quickly while keeping both a physical and an emotional balance in chaotic situations. The way they carry themselves conveys leadership to those around them.

Emotional intelligence or E.Q. has become a widely recognized and used phrase in recent years, speaking to a set of competencies that Daniel Goleman defined as self-awareness, self-regulation, motivation, empathy and social skills.[126] Common wisdom still seems to have it that the development of those competencies concludes in our early twenties — along with most of our other developmental processes. As a result, many of us are a bit startled as adults to discover that after adolescence we still have phases to go through; hitting the age of twenty-one does not really make one an emotional adult.

Emotional maturity is rooted in the capacity for love. Such capacity begins with the capability for intimacy in relationships, that willingness to deeply see and be seen by another. It extends into the ability to make and honor commitments due to a "mutual interpenetration of emotion and will,"[127] even when such commitments call for sacrifice or compromise. It grows, according to psychologist Erik Erikson, in turn into generativity, the "readiness to care for and nurture the next generation and the life conditions and resources of all kinds they will need to become generative."[128] With such capacity for love, emotional maturity is recognizable by a profound kind of tender comfortableness — inside our own skin and with others. A team that has worked well together for a long time will often show this kind of comfort and ease with one another.

On the autonomy side, emotional maturity includes the capacity for independence, a willingness to take action as a free agent. It offers the ability to hold clear boundaries, to withstand negative judgments without capitulating. Most important for leaders, it enables them to withstand the high levels of anxiety that those around them may experience, without letting go of their clarity or compassion.

On the connection side, emotional maturity means the willingness to affiliate with others, to freely initiate and sustain loving relationships. In the new space that happens when these two merge, we find what Rabbi Edwin Friedman describes as the person who can "self-differentiate without losing connection."

The unique monsters for emotional maturity are many and varied. Mentioned earlier were ego (a need to always be right or on top), narcissism (fascination with oneself), insecurity (often accompanied by a lack of self-awareness) and absence of impulse control (especially an inability to control one's temper). Another emotional monster can be a learned response to life's demands that got us through a difficult childhood. This response may be nearly invisible to us, but have become quite counterproductive for us as adults.

The icon for emotional maturity combines two important symbols. The circle represents boundaries and autonomy and the cross represents relationship.

 EMOTIONAL MATURITY

Autonomy : capacity for independence, willingness to take action as free agent.

Connection : capacity to affiliate, freely initiate and sustain loving relationships with others, and with the world around you.

Monsters : ego, need to be right, narcissism, insecurity, anger, absence of impulse control, childhood survival techniques.

Moral Maturity

For many of us, moral maturity appears a bit remote, something ministers, rabbis, mullahs, priests, lawyers and judges need to develop so that the rest of us can count on them to sort out issues. We fail to make the connection between moral development and the day-to-day choices we make. This lack of a moral discourse, a frequent conversation about moral and ethical issues, makes it harder for people to develop moral maturity.

The dictionary defines moral as "pertaining to the discernment of good and evil." Robert Kegan notes:

> But being able to think this way is not just a discrete skill, it is an active demonstration of a mind that can stand enough apart from its own opinions, values, rules and definitions to avoid being completely identified with them. It is able to keep from feeling that the whole self has been violated when its opinions, values, rules or definitions are challenged.[129]

Significantly, what he is actually discussing here is not moral maturity, but emotional maturity. These two domains mirror one another in profound ways. Neuroscientists conducting brain imaging find that moral issues light up parts of our most primitive emotion centers. "Morality is not a superficial thing that we added on very late in our evolution," according to Frans de Waal, author of *Chimpanzee Politics*. "It relates to very old affectionate and affiliative tendencies that we have as a species, and that we share with all sorts of animals."[130] Making the distinctions necessary to moral maturity, to high-level ethical reasoning, thus requires, on the autonomy side, the ability to step out from being embedded in one's own primitive emotional reactions.

James Fowler, in his careful synthesis of emotional, moral and spiritual development, *Stages of Faith*, notes that moral development further requires that people have had the "experience of *sustained responsibility for the welfare of others*, and the experience of making and living with irreversible moral choices."[131] With such experiences, the capacity to deeply process moral issues develops, balancing the need for both fairness and justice with the need for compassion.

Combining that capacity with the necessary level of intellectual maturity (thinking in whole systems), Fowler observes, leads to the kind of mature processing that allows one to think in terms of "principles of justice that can claim universal validity."[132]

> The formulation of and action in terms of universalizable moral principles, therefore, require a moral imagination informed enough and detached enough from one's own interests to accurately take the perspective of every person or group affected by a policy or action being considered.[133]

On the autonomy side, moral maturity reflects both the ability to move beyond one's own reactions and the capacity to see clearly and hold fast to those universal moral principles when those around us are no longer so inclined. On the connection side, it moves beyond taking the other's perspective to actively staying in dialogue with those whose moral values or principles are different.

Here we begin to see how these domains interweave and overlap. The "moral imagination" required for the highest levels of moral maturity must be informed and nourished by high levels of intellectual and emotional development. At its finest, when autonomy and connection merge, moral maturity invites the capacity for forgiveness and even reconciliation without losing sight of accountability. It weaves a finely nuanced balance between responsibility and compassion, and creates a structure that honors our needs for both independence and intimacy.

When Sherron Watkins became aware of the accounting practices that ultimately led to the largest bankruptcy in U.S. history, her reaction was "I wasn't going to be able to live with myself, just slink off and find another job. I felt I had to say something, I had to do something."[134] Through memos and meetings, she worked hard to maintain the connections, hoping as VP of Corporate Development, she could persuade the rest of Enron's leadership the company was in terrible jeopardy and needed to take strong and immediate steps to restore its integrity. Today, she is philosophic about the career costs — that other companies might perceive it dangerous to hire her, should Enron completely go under. She also sees new opportunities in the corporate boards that are now seeking training in how to recognize and actively prevent such scandals in the future.[135] Intellectual, emotional and moral maturity clearly enhance her leadership.

The monsters in the moral maturity domain are often subtle and elusive. Most often they are driven by emotional issues. Greed, for example, the rapacious desire for more of everything, is often driven by deeply rooted fear that we won't be okay without lots of material "stuff," an attempt to fill an emotional void that can really only be filled (or healed) by love. The kind of life fatigue that prevents us from asking the hard questions — "Is this really the right thing to be doing?" — in the press of getting through our day is another kind of moral monster.

Intellectual self-justification can be a moral monster as well, especially when it involves focusing on the parts instead of stewardship for the whole. That kind of thinking is often the path by which ordinary citizens get caught up in participating in large-scale evil, as did Germans in World War II. Apathy, a deadly moral monster, often travels in a herd along with self-justification and dishonesty. Apathy is essentially a failure to care enough to look at the moral implications of our own or others' behavior. Dishonesty is when we consciously or unconsciously ignore the consequences of that behavior or pretend that it is okay despite obvious negative consequences to others.

The symbol of the square illustrates stability, constancy, firmness and strength, the building block of social structure. Moral maturity is one of those building blocks.

 MORAL MATURITY

Autonomy : capacity to hold fast to moral course or compass when others aren't.

Connection : capacity to stay in dialogue with those whose moral values are different, to see commonality in values.

Monsters : greed, life fatigue, dishonesty, self-justification, apathy.

Spiritual Maturity

In conversations about leadership, spiritual maturity is the least frequently explored attribute. Yet, clearly, the people recognized as great leaders in the second half of the twentieth century — Gandhi, Martin Luther King Jr., the Dalai Lama, Mother Teresa, Jimmy Carter, Nelson Mandela and others — all led or lead from their spiritual and moral authority rather than from any traditional power base. Perhaps this is because, as the noted biologist Edward O. Wilson observes,

People need a sacred narrative. They must have a sense of larger purpose, in one form or another, however intellectualized. They will refuse to yield to the despair of animal mortality.[136]

The leaders who provide this sacred narrative for us are, in the end, the ones who move us most deeply.

Spiritual maturity seems like an exalted state to have reached, one that feels quite far away to the average person exploring a leadership journey. Yet, as in the other domains, spiritual development moves through stages. A useful question to ask is whether the internal and external conversation about such development is alive and well rather than whether we will somehow make it to "the top." Fowler notes in *Stages of Faith*:

> For persons in a given stage at the right time for their lives, the task is the full realization and integration of the strengths and graces of that stage rather than rushing on to the next stage. Each stage has the potential for wholeness, grace and integrity and for strengths sufficient for either life's blows or blessings.[137]

At the same time, it is valuable for the conversation that we define what spiritual maturity ultimately looks, sounds and feels like. As Fowler describes it,

> The rare persons who may be described at this stage have a special grace that makes them seem more lucid, more simple, and yet somehow more fully human than the rest of us. Their community is universal in extent. ... Their felt sense of an ultimate environment is inclusive of all being ... [and their lives are] a disciplined, activist *incarnation* — a making real and tangible — of the imperatives of absolute love and justice.[138]

Here again we clearly see those developmental poles coming together and opening a new space, a space not always visible to others. Inside that space lives a profoundly felt gratitude, a deeply sensed joy in living and a wholeness fed by hope. Inside that space there lives, as well, a transcendence of many of the issues of daily life that subtly or not so subtly constrain the rest of us.

Spiritual maturity ultimately frees us of the burden of concern for how others assess us and asks us instead to assess ourselves in the light of what is being asked of us, what needs to be done, what is in the highest interests of the greatest number of people. It asks us to step up to stewardship for the planet.[139] It asks us to create new stories of how life could be, to, as Fowler writes, "spend and be spent"[140] through living *now* in ways that represent the best of our future. Barbara Waugh's ongoing efforts to get HP to think about the world's poor as they develop business strategy — part of a larger conversation about sustainable development that is occurring in a surprising number of corporate offices today — illustrate some of the new stories that are emerging.[141]

As we develop, autonomy in spiritual development looks more and more like the capacity to develop and maintain a spiritual discipline, a consistent set of personal practices that increase one's ability to discern where spirit is leading. Connection is both the capacity to stay connected to that spirit, that source of strength and inspiration, and the profound desire to be of service, to utilize and return the gifts that life has offered.

The monsters of spiritual maturity are perhaps the most elusive for most of us. Jung is said to have observed that "every crisis over the age of forty is a spiritual crisis." As we noted earlier, depression may be the most common form that spiritual monsters take in the work world, and it is usually perceived as emotional rather than spiritual. Yet the inability to make one's life meaningful, to see value in it, is fundamentally a crisis of the spirit. There is also a monster of secrecy about our need for a spiritual life that afflicts many in the workplace — we cannot or will not admit to our spiritual yearning, that desire to be part of something larger than ourselves.

Two other significant spiritual monsters, both of which clearly overlap with the emotional, are addiction and cynicism. Addiction is the yearning for transcendence that Julio Olalla describes channeled into a physical or material experience — drugs and alcohol, sex, consumerism, gambling, etc. Cynicism is the failure to recognize anything greater than one's own selfish needs, and hence an inability to make meaning with any greatness attached to it.

The spiral represents a journey and growth in almost every culture. It holds both a sense of ongoing motion and an upward movement, reaching towards something higher.

 SPIRITUAL MATURITY

Autonomy : capacity to develop and maintain a spiritual discipline, personal spiritual practices that allow you to discern where spirit leads you.

Connection : capacity to stay connected to one's spiritual source and a profound desire to utilize and return the gifts life has offered.

Monsters : depression, secrecy, addiction, cynicism.

Elderhood

Within these four domains, we begin to see a vision of our maturity and our elderhood: it is a time of increasing integrity and grace, when issues of ego and pride can be transcended in service to something far greater.

A little-known story about George Washington powerfully illustrates such elderhood. When the Revolutionary War ended, Washington retired as commander-in-chief and went home. Congress, distracted by lack of funds and many competing factions, was slow to attend to the needs of battle-weary officers and soldiers who had fought and never been paid. Furious at this cavalier treatment, Continental Army officers convened a meeting at their postwar headquarters in Newburgh, New York. They threatened insurrection and offered to declare Washington king if he would join them and march on the capital.

> Washington denounced the proceedings as "irregular and disorderly" before convening his own gathering, at which he tried to flatter his sullen audience with visions of grateful posterity.
>
> None of this had much effect until the general retrieved from his pocket a congressional message promising early redress of legitimate complaints. He fumbled with the paper for a few seconds, then reached again into his coat to fetch a pair of eyeglasses. Begging the indulgence of his men, he explained to a stunned audience, "I have already grown gray in the service of my country. I am now going blind." Instantly, rebellion melted into tears. [142]

This simple act of admitting a weakness he had long hidden reminded the officers of the meaning of sacrifices they had made. The decision was made to give Congress another chance and a few weeks later the troops were paid. Washington's ability to not be seduced by the promise of great power, but to gently disarm those who were about to stray from their own moral and spiritual values, was an extraordinary gift to the young nation.

Facing Our Monsters

Each person's leadership story is about facing his monsters, in whatever domain they may be. Often, in stories — and in real life — the heroes get stuck in the pit. They are afraid to meet the monster. The monster is actually a projection of the fears they need to confront in order to learn, grow and develop maturity. They cannot accept uncertainty or allow change. They resist the normal developmental stages in some or all of the domains we've just discussed.

Every stage is a journey with its own monsters and a return to a higher maturity. The stages themselves, in fact, may be the monster that must be confronted in order for the story to move forward. Any time we observe a manager who seems frozen in place, unable to make the decisions that will move business forward, we are seeing someone stuck in the pit, confronted by internal monsters.

Similarly, someone who substitutes busy-ness for productivity, who fights any loss of control yet can not seem to move product out the door, is caught by a monster, stuck in the pit. Those workers whose doors are always closed may be seeking quiet to get work done or hiding from coworkers, afraid they will be found out — stuck in the pit. In each case, fear is the monster driving their behavior.

Any stage change, any growth process inevitably produces stress and anxiety. If we can no longer be who we were, who can we be? How do we re-create ourselves and where on the poles of our need for autonomy and connection will we rest? The resulting anxiety can be crippling if not fully understood. The philosopher Peter Koestenbaum, one of the few business writers to address leadership maturity, comments that:

Kierkegaard wrote that the most common form of despair occurs when one does not choose or "will" to be oneself — when a person is "another than himself." The opposite of despair is "the will to be that self which one truly is." That's the experience of anxiety. It is choosing life in the face of death; it is the experience of thought becoming action, reflection becoming behavior, and theory becoming practice. Anxiety is pure energy.[143]

He further observes that facing our anxiety is the mark of maturity, and that only in facing it can we move ourselves toward the self-knowledge that builds character and inner strength. "The practical formula: go where the pain is."[144] This is, indeed, how we face the monsters.

One of the biggest monsters that leaders must potentially face is their perfectionism, the temptation to be performers rather than learners. This demonstrates the power, once again, of story. *It is the story we hold about our journey that lets us face our monsters*. It is not so much that leaders should set these concepts of maturity as goals that have to be achieved. Instead, they can — and must — build stories for themselves that *allow* for these levels of growth and maturity, stories that encourage such striving, stories that enhance one's sense of possibility for integrity and wholeness and invite others to participate as well.

"The real quest is for the story; what story is worth your life?"[145] When leaders have the story worth their lives, they can summon the courage, the curiosity and the resilience to conquer some monsters and make peace with others. They live the story.

In 1985, Jack Stack, manager of the diesel-engine rebuilding facility Springfield Remanufacturing, heard that his plant was to be closed. Recognizing the impact it would have on the community of Springfield, Missouri, he invited the workers to join him in a leveraged buyout. To everyone's astonishment, their offer was accepted. Stack realized that, in order to succeed, everyone in the plant would need to understand what he called "The Great Game of Business." Classes were set up on the plant floor, and employees came to understand how to read a balance sheet and which line on that balance sheet their work specifically impacted. A real-time balance sheet was put together out of an old basketball scoring system and hung on the plant floor, so people could see how what they did mattered. Twenty years later, Springfield Remanufacturing is thriving. Because "open book management" reflected the faith Stack had in people, it became the story worth his life, and is now also a way of life in many other companies.[146]

This is the profound and inevitable story of maturity. We lose the focus that drove our youthful selves to lead by constantly doing, and slowly become grown-up leaders, people whose leading is through their being. We become people who *are* their stories, and whose stories are, indeed, worth their lives.

Conclusion: Monsters Abound

Monsters exist in all domains of life — emotional, intellectual, moral and spiritual — and must be faced. Facing them builds a story of maturity. While we lose the narrow focus that drove our youthful selves to lead by constantly doing, slowly we gain a grown-up leader in its place. We become a leader whose leading is through our *being*, the kind of person we have become. When we each become a person who *is* our story, that story is, indeed, worth a lifetime.

The purpose of the journey in every story, be it large or small, is, through speaking the truth and pointing to hope, to face our anxieties and take some steps toward wisdom and maturity. To do that, we need to know what wisdom and maturity look, sound and feel like. Yet these are images and conversations that seem sadly lacking — in the workplace, at home and in our political and religious communities. The definitions of maturity offered here can jumpstart our conversations about leadership.

As we take our hero's journey, each of us must build a leadership story that opens the possibility of wisdom in all domains. We must face the monsters, the fears that impede our movement towards maturity, all along the way. How we do that depends on who we are and where we are on our journey — in the preparation, in the pit or on the return. In every case, the purpose of the journey is to move ourselves toward wisdom, wholeness and completion. Inevitably, we experience profound transitional moments, moments that are defining "inflection points" for us. These are the *wormhole experiences*, the ones that catapult us to a different time and place in our own awareness and capacity as leaders. We will look next at those experiences to understand how they change our lives.

LEADERSHIP IS LOVE MADE VISIBLE
DR. DARYA FUNCHES
OF REAP™ CONSULTING

Darya Funches is founder and CEO of The REAP Gallery Unlimited Corporation and former Chair of the Board of Directors of NTL Institute. She has over thirty years of experience in corporate and personal transformation, executive development and professional development of change agents and visionary leaders. In her roles as consultant, educator and developer of professionals in the field, she has conducted over 1500 seminars and led hundreds of seminars and consulting engagements for clients such as Atlantic Energy, AT&T companies, Eastman Kodak, Citicorp-Citibank, Ethicon Endosurgery, IBM, Board of Governors-Federal Reserve and many Federal agencies and non-profit organizations.

Darya was ahead of her time in asserting that, "you cannot lead others to a place you have not been yourself — at least in consciousness." Leaders who want to transform countries, corporations, communities and industries must transform themselves as part of creating what's new. Now she contends that "the science of use of self is the new technology on which the economies of the future will be based."

Darya has always been on the furthest edges of personal and leadership development. She sees where the story of Third Principle leadership takes us. Her observation that our "self" — who we are as human beings — is the tool we have with which to lead was quite powerful to me twenty years ago. Once again, I find her insights about leadership, love and paradox to be well ahead of most of us.

LISA MARSHALL: Darya, you are the person who introduced me to organizational development work, and we share some common beliefs about the nature of leadership and people's power to lead. How are you using the term leadership these days?

DARYA FUNCHES: Leadership is the capacity to bring from within oneself what is most needed for the self and the whole. Leadership is helping others bring out what sustains the self and the whole, so that all exist in a harmonious web of life. When I say "whole," I am referring to the large and small senses of the word. There is the wholeness of the universe and the wholeness of a particular situation.

Leadership is a quality that comes from within. It is not really a position or a role, although we have attempted to capture it as such in our organizational, religious and political lives. Some of the best leaders I've met during corporate transformation efforts did not even hold management positions. I don't even think that leadership always comes with a set of conscious followers. In other words, there may be no shared awareness of a "leadership-followership" relationship.

In its purest form, leadership leaves an opening for people to choose to join or connect with a particular thought or action. It doesn't assume a predisposed set of people who are elected or employed. You can exercise leadership by speaking out into a particular space without having been requested or assigned, except by one's own core design. So, all of us have the capacity to lead in different circumstances. Followers are people connecting into the same wave that they experience as being initiated by the leader. Both followers and leaders are responding to their inner guidance.

We see examples of leadership that is initiated without followers in ideas "borrowed" or taken by this country from Native American tribes. They are the leaders behind some of our symbols and ideas about democracy. Similarly, we see and hear the creativity of

African American youths from city streets in mainstream advertising and communications. We even see this dynamic in the movie *Forrest Gump*. Forrest starts on a long run for his own needs and ends up with numerous followers. A person can be a thought leader, initiating a change in consciousness in a country, and not begin with organizing or leading others, so to speak.

LM: What, in your mind, is the internal drive to lead?

DF: Each of us has an inner configuration that has its own frequency and generates its own impulses. The drive or call that comes from that matrix of a person is his or her core design. We each have our own internal design that is forever unfolding and evolving. Some aspects of it are ancestral, some are from personality, and some are spiritual, based on our choices and purposes for living in this particular lifetime. We can evolve to follow that inner guidance rather than doing what is prescribed or expected by others. This inner, spiritual drive is just as compelling, if not more compelling, than our physiological needs.

LM: What is its source?

DF: Earlier, you asked, "Why does one person respond to the call to leadership in a particular situation and another person does not?" I would answer with the following question: "Why should the lights in your house come on because I switched on the lights in mine?" People's spirits are activated differently because everybody is wired differently. Our houses may be on the same block, yet my experience of what is going on in my house gets me to turn on the lights, while the experience you have and the choice you make in your house is different.

LM: When do you know you've received the call to leadership?

DF: When your telephone rings, you know you are receiving a call. There is a connection within you, between you and your inner self, and between you and Creator that is very much like the telephone call. *You have to know who you are to recognize this voice from within.* On the journey to knowing the self, there are transformations along the way, bringing you closer and closer to recognition of your own design.

Then, all of a sudden, you find yourself, or some aspect of the self, not fully recognized. By the way, that phrase *all of a sudden* often characterizes the inner experience of transformation. Most of the leaders and transformers I interviewed for my dissertation [1993] used the term *all of a sudden* when describing their stories of personal and organizational transformation.[147]

It intrigues me that we have accepted ways of knowing that are external, such as accepting the fact that the telephone is ringing as a call. When we hear or feel that ringing within ourselves, however, we sometimes question its validity. We question whether there is a call or just our imagination. We question who is calling.

In some circles, people do not discuss or accept as true what is spiritual and internally discernable. In those circles, people who are grounded in listening to spirit and the call from within may be seen as unstable, narcissistic, and/or delusional. In other circles, the ability to hear Spirit, and act in accordance with the calls we hear from within, is a sign of advanced human development, maturity and social responsibility.

I received such a call in the early 1980s. I had become increasingly aware of a need to deepen and accelerate the ways of working with organizational and leadership development and change. The spiritual, political, cultural, psychological and social parts of my life began to talk to one another, so to speak. That's when I wrote "Three Gifts of the Organization Development Practitioner," [1989] an article about discernment, heart and presence.[148]

Those three gifts were my way of talking about use of self as an instrument of change and transformation. The work on use of self initially came from Spirit *through* me. Around the same time, I also received guidance about a model for creating reality. I worked on these ideas for several years, and they formed the basis of my work in transformation.

Sometimes, when I am guided by Spirit to take a leap or make a move, I respond with "You talkin' to me?" Yet, as a result of my questions, prayers and listening in the early eighties, what unfolded was a journey so compelling that it has driven my life for at least seventeen years. Now I am working with the "Three Gifts" as tools for leadership and transformation for everyone, not just change agents and managers.

LM: When do you recognize the call in someone else? How?

DF: The fires from within burn just a bit brighter in someone who is following his/her calling. If we look, we can probably see it. What do you see? That depends on how well you've developed your gift of discernment. When they are working in the area of their calling, you notice their magnetism and their radiance.

We all have the capacity for leadership. Our callings are triggered by different situations. Some people choose to jump over the transformational bar; some back up from it, won't stand up and speak their truth. As much as anything, I've come to recognize that I'm in the "truth" business.

LM: How do you know the call has been answered?

DF: If you were to apply your ways of knowing things on a physical level to the ways of knowing about the call, you would answer this question. This is one of the things I do with myself and with leaders. I help them refine that knowingness. We need to turn up the volume on that inner world, these inner ways of seeing and knowing. I'm working on doing this with the book version of "Three Gifts."

Having a vision of the future is one of these inner ways of knowing. The term *vision*, however, may be one of the most misused terms in corporate life. From the spiritual perspective, a vision is a bona fide personal experience. To the visionary, it is as real as the chair in your house. You're answering the call when you do what is shown to you in a vision, when you do what you are led to do by the inner impulses of your soul's design.

So how do you know you have answered the call? You know because you experience it, the same way you know the phone just rang. It is the same way you know you have answered the body's quest for water by drinking some. When we have learned to depend on external sources of knowing, it can be a challenge to get to this inner knowing. Sometimes it takes the assistance of someone who has already traveled the path. The work is well worth the journey.

LM: What do you as a leader need from others in order to be effective? What roles do you need them to play?

DF: If I am leading based on an inner call, I'm jumping into a situation from the inside out. I don't need anything from others except to hear what I'm saying and hear what their inner voices are telling them. I need something in order for us to accomplish something *together*, but I don't need anything from them in order to use myself as a leader if it's my inner calling.

If I think about a group that asks me to lead, then I need commitment, an energy that's equivalent, making it clear that we're all putting something on the table. So I want a commitment and realization that we're in it together, no jumping ship. At different levels of involvement and in different roles, we commit. I want a lot of truth. I find that lies can be pervasive and destructive in organizational life. Uncovering the truth can be uncomfortable *and* liberating. And I love to have fun. Leading a major shift or change can be fun, a supreme adventure of the highest order, full of passion, love, anxiety, excitement and laughter.

LM: Describe for me your own leadership journey, please.

DF: As an African American woman who is conceptual and practical, visionary and action-oriented, creative and concrete, spiritual and material, understanding my own presence has been a piece of work. Sometimes I don't fit management's picture of a person they would call for expertise, since I am not a white male. I've had clients who felt I was the best at what they needed who also felt ambivalent about my presence.

In a way, it's all summed up by my birth story. I was born in 1949, when blacks were not allowed to be born in hospitals in Mississippi. My parents were moving from Chicago to Texas. Dad went early and Mama went to Mississippi to be with her mother for my birth. Having had her first child in a hospital in Chicago, she wasn't going to settle for less the second time, so she worked out an arrangement with a white doctor for her baby to be born secretly in the local white hospital, which was called King's Daughters Hospital.

When the time came for her to deliver, the white nurses weren't ready to take her down the hall to the delivery room for fear that people would see her. She got up out of the bed and said, "I'm going to have this baby in the hall if you don't take me." So they threw a sheet over her and rolled her down the hall. So this little change agent came in the back door! We come forth any way — back door, front door, side door — and rise to some occasion. A spark in all of us arises eventually.

LM: What do you think is the destination?

DF: My intention is to develop new forms of leadership and organization for the twenty-first century. In this moment, it's where

I feel the call — and I don't know how it plays out. There were times when I've felt I'd best serve from another dimension. I've been ahead of my time. The world was a little less ready. Now people may be more ready to work with the connections between business, science and spirit — between the spiritual and material worlds — in organizations.

LM: What have been your most transformational experiences as a leader?

DF: My initiation into motherhood. Becoming a mother was probably my greatest transformation. People who never take that journey (having and/or raising kids) have to develop the heart aspect of leadership in a different manner.

The heart is one of the most maturing aspects of growing up; it is the seat of love/wisdom. In the U.S., our thinking tends to equate the heart with emotion, and that's not what I mean. I mean that the heart is the aspect of the connectedness of all things; the wholeness that I talk about is very much seated in the maturity of the heart.

LM: What gets in the way of your leadership?

DF: Hesitation can get in the way. Hearing the phone and not answering it. Not checking the inner voice mail, not responding. I've been given a lot of visions, a lot of dreams. Sometimes I have to wait to know how it all fits together, how the dots connect. I may wait or fumble around in the dark for a while. At other times, the message is compelling and clear and I act immediately. I check internally: Is *now* the time?

Also, attempts to control things too much get in the way. I have to allow the space for the clarity to come from within. I experiment. I have to be in the flow. That's part of what my leadership is about. If it's not fun, then something's missing, something's wrong and you're not in the flow.

LM: What dilemmas cause you the greatest concern?

DF: The Organization Development Network's Annual Conference had "Paradox" as its theme in 1997. I did the closing keynote. In it, I gave my view of paradox: "Paradox is the last illusion before the reality of wholeness." So, I suppose I am saying to you, if there is a dilemma, it's that we even conceive of ourselves as leading anything. How can we lead that which already exists in its absolute form of wholeness?

If anything, a leader is leading a movement in perception that has been based on separation rather than wholeness. If you're *in* the absolute wholeness, the absolute truth of it, you can't conceive of yourself as leading anything. At my best, what I am is being the wholeness that I know exists. That's the only way out of that dilemma or the paradox: being the wholeness.

LM: How have you evolved or matured as a leader?

DF: I understand now how important it is to have one's love made visible. Part of leadership's role is making love apparent in larger and larger and larger systems. My work, of course, focuses on a particular type of leadership, visionary leadership for transformation and creating new realities. A visionary leader helps to bring the design — the highest potential — within the core of an organism into physical reality.

That's also how I've evolved or matured. That's how I lead myself, so to speak. I'm responsible to the whole, but not responsible for everyone's choices. I do my "whole" and let it go. I ask more of spirit, "What is it that you want me to do? Where do I need to be/go? Place me where you want me to be."

LM: How haven't you?

DF: Sometimes there is a part of me that is still tempted to make something happen and impose my will before I know where I am most needed. I remind myself, "Be still and know that God is within me and all around me. Listen."

There is always a place for the way I use my abilities and gifts — a place where my contributions are needed, just as there is for all of us.

METAMORPHOSIS

GROWING TOWARD ARRIVAL
WORMHOLES AND METAMORPHOSIS

> *I wouldn't give a fig*
> *for the simplicity this side of complexity,*
> *but I would give my life*
> *for the simplicity on the other side of complexity.*
>
> ~ OLIVER WENDELL HOLMES

Inherent in the hero's journey is the notion of a change, a metamorphosis. It's what is required to face down monsters, bring anxiety under control and successfully climb out of the pit.

Metamorphosis means "a transformation, as if by magic or sorcery, a marked change in appearance, character, condition or function." The caterpillar spins a cocoon, hides inside and returns a butterfly. The concept of the wormhole is a way to describe this experience, that tunnel in the fabric of space-time through which the leader vaults into a new way of thinking and being. It fits the metaphor of an almost magical (and often bewildering) change, one that takes someone to an utterly different place and time than was expected.

Four distinct categories of wormhole showed up in my conversations with leaders, each with its own unique set of characteristics:

+ Accepting the call,
+ Letting go of doing it alone,
+ Living under the microscope, and
+ Not having all the answers.

Not everyone went through all of these, but all went through at least one. All such experiences, however, have several elements in common. They each trigger abrupt discontinuity, a stunning *pattern interrupt* for the person who undergoes them. Each has a humbling impact. The leader who experiences them is knocked off whatever developmental pole he was resting on and endures a period of uncertainty, of not quite knowing himself, before the old identity can be transcended and included in a new, fuller, richer one. This is exactly the metamorphosis from caterpillar to butterfly Mort Meyerson described earlier.

Often this transition, this wormhole experience, is swallowed up in a crisis of some kind, so that the change, though felt as dramatic, is really only understood retrospectively. For this reason, wormhole experiences may be more clearly perceived by those around the leader than by that leader herself. Observers experience a deeply changed person, one who acts visibly differently than she did before. Observers may be impacted as well, deeply moved by such visible growth, and can find their loyalty to that leader increased.

First Wormhole: Accepting the Call

For some people, just accepting that they *are* leaders, that others perceive them that way, and that it is time to accept their leadership role is a stunning experience. It requires a dramatically different sense of self than the one they previously carried. When they come to understand that they are indeed called to lead, here and now, their world is never quite the same again. For one person, it is the moment when a question is asked and all heads turn toward her for the answer. For another, it may be the moment of realizing that if there's bad news to be given, he would rather be the one to give it.

When the call is accepted, the twin gifts of clarity and compassion begin to expand. Suddenly that person is capable of facing the monsters of self-doubt and resignation, the monsters of insufficiency and the monsters that imply something is hopeless, that no one will follow her. Suddenly she finds herself more focused on what needs to be done than on who should do it. She begins to trust her own "knowing," and to connect with what others are experiencing. Suddenly a new story begins.

In the leadership research, one leader telling of his leadership journey spoke of a time when he was eleven or twelve and his coach asked him for his opinion of the team. "He listened, and included me in the decision. Boy, once you get that confidence from someone like that, you just want to do more and more to get it."[149] The energizing realization that what we do matters, to a coach, to a team, to family or colleagues, can make all the difference in the world.

Second Wormhole: Letting Go of Doing It Alone

The second wormhole is the experience of facing that we can't go it alone. (Or as one young leader put it, you can't "wear the red underwear [Superman's costume] forever."[150]) It may be that the projects get too big or the complexity too great; the result is the same. We recognize that we can't think through the whole situation alone, that others are needed to succeed, not just to keep from feeling lonely.

There is often a major crisis of confidence when young, technically gifted leaders begin to realize that they can no longer hold the plans inside their head because the project's scope has expanded beyond their capacity. This may seem blindingly obvious, but for many young leaders, it is a painful moment, and feels like failure: "I should have been able to do it myself. How can I be a leader if I need other people?"

There are two major learnings from this wormhole experience. One is that we need our Merry Many — colleagues, teammates, whoever travels with us on the journey. Developing them takes time and conversation. To develop them, leaders need to have been intentional, as David Whyte notes, about keeping five key conversations alive inside and outside their organizations:

- The conversation about what is over the horizon, what the future holds (critical to building the living story);

- The conversation with customers or constituents about what they want and need (what the near-term story holds);
- The conversation among all the disparate parts of the organization, the one that builds bridges, creates synergy and gets good work done;
- The conversation amongst colleagues and peers, so that knowledge is managed and shared; and
- The conversations inside each mind and heart in the organization that build commitment and passion for the work at hand.[151]

With those conversations alive and well in the organization, the merry many stay involved and committed. Without those conversations, their sense of their own leadership contribution dies. And so does their commitment.

The other learning is that a good story will serve powerfully when the scope exceeds *plan-ability*. In today's fluid geopolitical, social, governmental and business environments, we increasingly run the risk of executing plans that are no longer relevant, even if they are still are doable. Peter Drucker is said to have commented, "There is nothing more pathetic than seeing something done well that need not be done at all." By building a story first, we can keep focused on what is relevant, what *should* be done. Then we can do our short-term planning with some confidence that we're staying on point. And because our leadership stories are living stories, they will evolve.

Third Wormhole: Living Under the Microscope

There are many tales of how an off-hand remark by the CEO results in a newly refurbished cafeteria (not her intention at all), or about the VP who has a fight with his wife, comes to work in a bad mood and trashes the new sales training program, utterly demoralizing the people who developed it (who don't know enough to ignore his temporary grumpiness). A reality of leadership is that one is *watched*. People study every move and every word. Then they attempt to interpret. A leader's perceived mood becomes the organization's mood. In a profound way, a leader's "self" is not just his anymore. It belongs to everyone. The higher one goes in an organization, the truer this is.

General Lucius Theus, one of the famed Tuskegee airmen, told this story about receiving his promotion to general. "All of a sudden, I realized that my words were the equivalent of issuing a command. This came sharply into focus when I was about to move. I asked when I would be going. 'Sir, you will be going when you wish to be going!' I immediately said to myself, 'I must be very careful to be sure I do only what I intend, in the manner I intend to do it.' Because it had such impact, it had to be as it should have been, nothing wrong."[152]

One must become exquisitely aware of one's own behavior and its impact. Carly Fiorina, CEO of Hewlett-Packard, is quoted as saying that, as CEO, "You may as well pay attention to your behavior; everyone else is." That behavior is what tells people, for example, whether their *yeses* can truly be promises, because they know whether they're allowed to say *no* to requests if they have to. And there is no value to a *yes* if one is not allowed to say *no*. The leader is the one who keeps that value in the currency of the group or organization — or erodes it. She models keeping promises and allowing people to tell the truth. She makes it clear that discipline matters by starting and ending meetings on time and by delivering on promises, making clear requests and expecting clear responses. And when other people have promised, she holds them accountable.

When these behaviors are in place, the result is muscularity in the story, a robustness and congruence that make it clear: this story *will* happen. An unexpected side benefit can also be an increased degree of leverage in the organization: when a leader's part of the organization honors its commitments, he stands on much firmer ground when insisting that others do likewise. After a three-year effort to install higher levels of discipline and accountability in his organization spear-headed by his mid-level managers, one general manager at Intel found himself barking at the general manager of another division: "In my organization, we keep our promises. I expect the same of you." The other manager contritely agreed to keep his commitments. When consistency of discipline and accountability are the result of this wormhole, understanding that leaders live under the microscope can have unexpected benefits.

Fourth Wormhole: Not All the Answers

The fourth wormhole has to do with recognizing and accepting, even making peace with, the reality that we don't have all the answers and never will. This is because there are dark places, shadow sides, in ourselves, in others and in the situation that make it hard to see with clarity. To see in the shadows we need a new set of conversations that enable people to discern what questions need to be asked, what problems need to be solved. A *Sloan Management Review* article by Kate Sweetman commented that:

> Three new studies suggest that true leadership often lies in knowing how to embrace uncertainty. The research suggests that when companies fail to recognize the importance of uncertainty, employees disengage from the organization's efforts. Leaders who get the best results combine an ability to set inspiring goals and a willingness to admit that they don't know exactly how to accomplish those goals. It turns out that people working for managers who openly express uncertainty and who seek employee input in resolving ambiguous challenges are more satisfied with their jobs, more committed to and less cynical about their organizations, and more likely to identify with the companies they work for.[153]

This wormhole experience is thus about humbly accepting the limits of your knowing and learning to live with ambiguity and paradox. It is about learning to trust. It includes developing the ability to "understand the other's position on the other's own terms,"[154] as well as the capacity to "see conflict as a signal of our over-identification with a single system,"[155] and open ourselves up to new possibilities. This is the wormhole that most directly leads to leadership through presence, the act of getting work done by enabling others rather than through action of our own.

A leader who has experienced this fourth wormhole discovers that much of what she does is create and hold the container by designing and supporting processes through which good work can get done. No longer needing to know or control the outcome, she trusts that the processes they've put in place will produce the results needed. As described earlier, when Gene Krantz announced during the Apollo 13 crisis, "There will be no failure on my watch," leaders construct boundaries that hold the work in place so that it can happen. The boundaries include priorities, time and resources.

But leaders may not know the exact path to the outcome. That is for others to discover, the ones who will actually walk that path. Through their leadership presence, their being, these leaders contain anxiety within themselves, channel that "pure energy"[156] positively and allow people to focus on getting the work done.

Other Wormhole Experiences

Obviously, these are not the only possible wormhole experiences. Getting fired, the loss of loved ones through death or divorce, a deeply felt spiritual experience, nearly dying oneself, having to fire people, even an organizational collapse of some kind, can all precipitate a trip through the wormhole. What all such experiences have in common is the sense of a tectonic plate shift, after which life is never quite the same again.

Wormhole experiences demand courage of us. As Peter Koestenbaum says, "No significant decision — personal or organizational — has ever been undertaken without being attended by an existential crisis, or without a commitment to wade through anxiety, uncertainty and guilt."[157] Whether it is the hard work of choosing how to approach a layoff, where to allocate scarce resources or whether to take a new assignment, these profound decision-making experiences change us. In choosing to recognize our patterns of thinking and experiencing life, in opening up our beliefs about "what we deserve and what's possible,"[158] we take the risks that maturity requires and earn the right to lead others.

Notice that we can only will *ourselves* to change. Leading others does not mean changing them or even willing them to change. Other people must make their own choices; no one else can change them. As Koestenbaum notes, we do not motivate people with techniques:

> ...but by risking yourself with a personal, lifelong commitment to greatness — by demonstrating courage. You don't teach it so much as challenge it into existence. You cannot choose for others. All you can do is inform them that you cannot choose for them. In most cases, that in itself will be a strong motivator for the people whom you want to cultivate. The leader's role is less to heal or to help than to enlarge the capacity for responsible freedom.... Greatness comes with recognizing that your potential is limited only by how you choose, how you use your freedom, how resolute you are, how persistent you are — in short, by your attitude. And we are all free to choose our attitude.[159]

Wormhole experiences generate a profound shift in attitude, often bringing us to an acceptance of the fundamental truth that our story is our own. We can be trapped by it or enlarged by it. The decision is ours.

Ultimately, the changes that we go through that mature us as leaders have the paradoxical effect of simplifying us while increasing our embrace of ambiguity. We know ourselves — what we value, for what or for whom we will take a stand — and we have accepted both our own strengths and weaknesses. We increasingly know when to step up and when to step down and are comfortable with both. At the same time, we no longer need to simplify the world, to insist on a black and white, either/or reality. Perhaps as we make peace with our monsters — and in so doing, accept our own dark or shadow sides and admit our own weaknesses without empowering them — we have less of a need to see extremes and polarize the world into "them or us," "right or wrong" and even "failure or success."

As we break through those mindsets, the world of possibilities inevitably enlarges. We see the "both/and" of everything, and revel in breaking the barriers. What happens no longer is about us or because of us; we are simply participants. As a result, whole new levels of response and response-ability become available.[160] Inevitably, this is accompanied by a growing sense of the whole, a vastly deepening appreciation for the interconnectedness of all aspects of life. This is what is meant by *stewardship of the whole*. It is from this simpler state that we can reach maturity in our emotional, intellectual, moral and spiritual domains.

In 1974, General George Lee Butler was assigned to the Air Force Directorate of Plans and asked to prepare positions for the Strategic Arms Limitation Talks (SALT). As he began working, he realized that many of the issues around the Soviet nuclear threat were rooted in bureaucratic politics, not real assessments of strategic concerns. The more he came to understand American nuclear strategic planning, the more he questioned the underlying rationale.

When named commander of the Strategic Air Command in 1991, Butler drastically reduced the number of nuclear strike targets, convinced that the overkill strategies of the Cold War were no longer appropriate. When arms talks resumed, he openly urged negotiators to lower ceilings on nuclear weapons, a position that many believe resulted in his not being appointed Colin Powell's successor as Chairman of the Joint Chiefs of Staff. Since retiring, he has actively lobbied for an end to all nuclear weapons. Intellectual maturity allowed him to question our nuclear military strategy, emotional maturity gave him the courage to take the unpopular positions that his moral maturity required and spiritual maturity was reflected in his deep desire to be of service to the world by committing himself to preventing nuclear warfare.[161]

Conclusion: The Simplicity on the Other Side of Complexity

No leader has all these wormhole experiences. Some do grow gradually and comfortably into their roles, making their way with grace and ease. But sooner or later, all true leaders face their shadow sides, their monsters and own them as part of themselves. Those who experience a wormhole often comment that it constituted a potent course correction, a character change that probably would not have come about any other way. And probably no leader with any staying power escapes the fourth wormhole. True maturity in leadership requires that we indeed attain that "paradoxical mixture of personal humility and professional will"[162] that Jim Collins encountered in his work on companies that went from being good to great.

The Zen Buddhist teacher Adyashanti points out, "The mind cannot endure paradox; the heart can." What we inevitably sense in mature leaders, in people who have faced their monsters, is that their hearts are wholly engaged with life and no longer struggling with paradox. They have come to understand that it is indeed "the last illusion before the reality of wholeness."[163] As whole human beings, such leaders invite the wholeness in everyone.

OPEN-HEARTED LEADERSHIP
MARGARET WHEATLEY
OF THE BERKANA INSTITUTE

For many years, Meg Wheatley has been interested in seeing the world differently. She has wanted to see beyond the Western, mechanical view of the world and see what else might appear when the lens was changed. She's learned, just as Joel Barker predicted when he introduced us to paradigms years ago, that "problems that are impossible to solve with one paradigm may be easily solved with a different one."

As a speaker, consultant and writer for twenty-eight years, Meg has been inside most kinds of organizations, from the Girl Scouts to the U.S. Army, from Fortune 100 companies to small-town churches. She has also lived and worked in many different cultures and countries. She loves the diversity, and she loves even more the realization that around the world, we share a common human desire to live together more humanely and more harmoniously.

She has been applying the lens of living systems theory to organizations and communities, exploring the question: "How might we organize differently if we understood how Life organizes?" It has been an exploration that has helped her look into old patterns and problems and develop new and hopeful insights and practices. It has also increased her sense of wonder for life, and for the great capacity of the human spirit. I put this interview here both for Meg's implicit understanding of maturity and because her own journey has been one of increasing spiritual maturity, the hardest domain for many of us to comprehend.

LISA MARSHALL: Meg, I know you have a long-standing fascination with how chaos or complexity theory illuminates organizational behavior and a strong commitment to the power of conversation. Your latest book, *Turning to One Another*, deeply speaks to these issues. What's your current definition of leadership?

MARGARET WHEATLEY: I'm taking a very different approach to leadership these days, in my efforts to get global conversations going. To me, a leader is anyone who wants to help at this time. It's someone who takes action, has a willingness to see something that needs to be different and steps forward to do something about it. A leader is anyone willing to move from noticing and complaining to doing something. We're not looking at power or style; we're measuring leadership by action. It's a broad global approach: mothers trying to help the children in their village, nurses trying to bring about rudimentary healthcare, parents worrying about schools.

LM: What, in your mind, is the internal drive to lead? Why does someone want to "help at this time?"

MW: It's about having one's heart opened to something particular. It's in our hearts that our courage is found. The French word *coeur* means heart. Our energy to step out comes from something that has opened our hearts. The great organizations started among a few friends who noticed something that was intolerable to them. When you start from that place, you don't have to create meaning; meaning motivates you to step out. The heart opening is inexplicable to me, it's part of the way life works. I believe it to be evidence of a greater purpose, a deeper intelligence at work in the world.

It's intriguing how differently we all respond, the different things people are called by. We each find our own hero's journey. Yet for each hero, it's their courage that motivates, that triggers the story. We discover our story; we don't make it up. That's important, because it gets the egotism out of our way. "What wants to happen," a phrase I use a lot, comes from the *I Ching*, the ancient Chinese Book of Wisdom. That describes the story.

LM: What is the source of that desire to help?

MW: Our gifts don't come from us; they come through us. I'm clearly into the maximally servant leadership model. Our gifts are an offering to everyone else. The meaning of our lives is something we discover; it's dangerous to decide too fast what your purpose is. You close off to new information and to just being available.

LM: What was your first experience of, or discovery of, your ability to lead?

MW: I noticed very young (age seven) that my friends followed me. I didn't use that authority well.

LM: How has your gift changed over time?

MW: Life is about learning how to be a leader that is in service to everyone else. That takes decades.

LM: When do you know you've received the call to leadership?

MW: You notice what gets your attention, what won't leave your mind, that's your call. What issues are currently tapping you on the shoulder and saying "You're it"? In your life, what gives you true satisfaction, what comes so easily that you don't even notice? What do people say, "You always…"? That's part of your gift. We don't see what our gifts are because they're so easy.

LM: When do you recognize it in someone else? How?

MW: You recognize a quality of their passion, their energy, even if it's hard, there's some spark there. You see people who don't stop —

if one way doesn't work, they do it another. They have a kind of tenacity, persistence, flexibility of means. And you hear a deeper sense of purpose; they're not just doing it for themselves, they believe "This will be really good for humanity."

LM: How do you know the call has been answered?

MW: You never do know. That's what most spiritual teachings tell us: give up any attachment to outcomes. The energy to do the work doesn't come from succeeding, or even hope, it comes from a different place. It's simply the work that has to be done. That's what service is. It's not in expectation of outcomes or success.

LM: What do you as a leader need from others in order to be effective? What roles do you need them to play?

MW: I don't think about this "roles" stuff. To pay attention to it ahead of time doesn't work. If they're truly archetypal, we can assume the right people for the right roles will show up. So I focus on how we are going to get this work done. Archetypes are unavoidable, and helpful for recognizing that we all play different roles, but I wouldn't focus on it ahead of time. If it's good work, I just need to put out the call and the right people show up.

LM: Describe your own leadership journey.

MW: Mine has been a profoundly spiritual journey to get outside of my own ego, to not be held in thrall by ego dynamics (such as a search for fame, status, power, wealth). The images I'm holding now have nothing to do with traditional leadership, just service. This came to pass partly from growing up, and partly from becoming a Buddhist, understanding that it's the right journey for me in this lifetime. It's what I'm meant to be learning right now. I believe that as a whole culture, we're being called to step beyond our material obsessions and become more compassionate and generous.

How does that change happen? Things happen *to* you. They tell you. Pay attention to what's happening to you. Life works actively here, and it's really nice if you get it sooner rather than later. Although it doesn't matter when you get it, as long as you get it. It can come from a philosophical perspective, or a spiritual tradition, something that lets you see things in a bigger light, less moment-to-moment.

LM: What do you think leadership's destination is?

MW: This is personal theology for all of us. For me, it's to have an awakened mind, to really understand what life is.

LM: What gets in the way of your leadership?

MW: Ego is the first thing that gets in the way. Then there are the things of this world, like lack of sufficient resources, lack of time. Not having enough people present to catch the vision quickly enough. But these are all ego things. I see so many great projects, and I feel frustrated that there isn't enough time, money or people.

LM: What are the dilemmas that cause you the greatest concern?

MW: We have a principle here at the Berkana Institute: "If it gets hard, you've taken charge: give it back." If it feels challenging that's fine, but when it starts to feel like you're carrying the whole world on your shoulders, give it back. There's an obvious and wide line between taking responsibility and carrying the whole world on your shoulders. If you believe or recognize that this issue has nominated you, then you need to believe that others have been prepared too, and that you don't have to do it alone. This way has been prepared for you, but that doesn't mean assuming you alone know what needs to be done.

People just don't have an appropriate understanding of what's important to work on, they don't have a systems perspective. It's the underlying mental models that are quite problematic. We need to discover how to get the work done, not how to be right.

LM: What have been your most transformational experiences as a leader?

MW: There have been so many. I would describe them as experiencing the power of true synchronicities. Synchronicities are a measure of whether you're doing the right work. If they're there, you're doing the right work. The way opens. Living with synchronicities has transformed me.

The other kind of experience is the transformational meetings I've been in, where great work is being done through us. There's more and more of that happening. It's so different from anything we've ever experienced before.

LM: What do you understand about leadership now that you didn't five or ten years ago?

MW: Leadership for me has become a spiritual journey, it's the hero's journey told spiritually. I now know the journey, know the markers of whether I'm on the right path. We never get perfect, but we get very sensitive to when we're even slightly off the path. It's not that I'm going to be a saint, but I'm going to know much faster when I'm off the path.

LM: How have you evolved or matured?

MW: It's not about me. It is only about serving. I didn't know that even a year ago, and probably still don't fully know it in all its beauty. It's about just being present, and having developed a lens to decide what I'm going to notice. To notice when I feel anger, or fear or uncharitable. If you're not conscious, you atrophy.

I also understand that people have charisma when they're actually doing their right work. And a kind of spaciousness. As a follower, when you don't meet an ego in the leader, there's room to be you.

RETURN

X | WHERE ALL THE RIVERS MEET THE RETURN

> *The opposite of a true statement*
> *is a false statement,*
> *but the opposite of a profound truth*
> *can be another profound truth.*
>
> ~ NIELS BOHR

It is one of the fundamental mysteries of life that, at the cellular level, our bodies are always changing, old cells dying and new ones being created to replace them. It is estimated that each day, about 2 billion of the body's cells wear out and are replaced. And that every 15 to 30 days, the human body replaces the outermost layer of skin. Yet somehow, each of us retains a core self. Somehow we continue to look and be our *selves*, to experience and be experienced as a person, a character that lasts a lifetime. Just as we never step into the same river twice, so too on our leadership journey do we wake each morning to a renewed self that still maintains the shape and flow of the old. (Whether it *feels* like the same old self is no doubt a function of whether we're resting easily on one of the developmental poles or in the midst of transition.)

At the end of the great stories, the heroes return home, the same yet different. So it is on our leadership journey. This raises provocative questions for our stories about leadership: to what do we return? What is home, in this context? How are we the same? How different? Does returning home signify simply an ending or a new beginning as well? In what ways does the return also mean a giving back, a returning of that which we have received? What are the implications of the return for maturity? Are they related?

Ultimately, the home we return to is our self, the total, essential and particular being that we are, the pared-down core that has somehow remained as we moved through each of our cycles of autonomy and connection. Yet this self is not the one we had when we accepted our call and began our journey. We have undergone enormous transformation. To have returned home, this self of ours has lost its innocence and regained it, lost its ability to see the world with clear eyes and peaceful heart and regained it.

Returning Home

As an archetype, the return represents both maturity and acceptance of our own accountability and imperfection: "*We* are now the rulers of the kingdom." We may not be happy at the state of our realm, but our maturity enables a rebirth within that realm. We access the inner forces that enable truth-facing and renewal. We become less attached to specifics (whether a plan or a specific objective), instead accepting a broad point of view that recognizes the universality and wholeness inherent in life and experiencing a deep and spontaneous joy in living.[164]

The elusive, spiraling nature of our leadership journey is embodied in the word *return*, if we think of it as a *re-turn* or *to turn again*. While implying that one comes back to a place one has been before, this concept also hints that every return may actually also be a turn in a new direction. According to the American Heritage Dictionary, its Indo-European root cognate, *ter*, means "to rub, turn, with some derivatives referring to twisting, boring, drilling and piercing, and other derivatives referring to the rubbing of cereal grain to remove the husks." Surely we return from our leadership journeys feeling that we have been twisted, bored, drilled and pierced along the way, and, if we have truly grown as leaders, that much of our husks have been removed!

And to what do we bring our de-husked selves back? What constitutes the "home" self in our leadership journey? Is it the familiar? Our place of origin? Our refuge from the world? Our family? The noted educator Parker Palmer speaks of such a home-coming as being different from a normal homecoming in two ways:

First, it is inner, not outer. This home is not a place that we can own — but by the same token, we cannot be banned from it, and it cannot be stolen from us. No matter where we are or what condition we are in or how many obstacles are before us, we can always come back home through a simple inward turning.

Second, when we make that inward turn, the home we find is not a closed and parochial place in which we can hide…. In this home, we know ourselves not as isolated atoms threatened by otherness but as integral parts of the great web of life. In that knowing, we are taken beyond fear toward wholeness.[165]

This home self has also come to see its own possibilities in very different ways. If the journey has been successful, this self has seen how to become more fully its own. In maturity, it has embraced its calling as the "element to which it belongs."[166] No longer does such a self need to calculate, to willfully, exhaustively scheme and plan: "People plan because they can't see what is happening."[167] This new self *can* see again. It can participate in what wants and needs to happen. In maturity, it has indeed moved "beyond fear toward wholeness," has been enlarged and deepened, and has come to deeply know that there is always a place for it in the universe.

This kind of return reflects gaining some degree of wisdom and maturity, being capable of a deeper conversation with the world. In that conversation, paradox and ambiguity can now be embraced instead of feared. Autonomy and connection weave together. In that conversation, the energy of life is alive and well. Issues can be explored and lived in. New meaning can be discerned, new questions asked. We are capable of doing *and* being because our selves, our core beings and their values, have grown in their integrity. Doing and being are so deeply integrated that paradox can be explored in our hearts and tolerated in our minds.

When Paul Wieand was fired from Independence Bancorp, he was on his way to being one of the country's youngest CEOs. Suddenly, his world came crashing down around him. Driven for decades by an un-diagnosed learning disability, he had set out to prove he *was* smarter, more competent and capable than anyone else. Success, however, laid the groundwork for failure: he came to believe he was smarter, and stopped listening to others. Completely identified with his job, its loss threw him into freefall. Six months later he was hired to turn around a failing thrift and started again. The bank turn-around succeeded, but Wieand began to see that he was unhappy, that success was not feeding him in the way he had hoped.

When a new board member began to attack him, Wieand decided to retire at age 41. He went to Temple University to get a PhD and began coaching executives. But it was his work with acute schizophrenics during his residency that really produced the break-through for him:

> I saw that everyone — whether they're patients in a psych ward or executives in a corporation — wants the same things in life: to be recognized, to be cared for and to be given an opportunity to grow. And, if you're authentic and trustful, people will realize that, and they'll respond. Authenticity is contagious.[168]

Now, Wieand has set up the Center for Advanced Emotional Intelligence to help people at the top of organizations understand fully the emotional implications of their roles and truly step into leadership. How does he do it? By starting powerful conversations about emotions, the forces that drive decision-making and meaning-making as well as our thought processes and our interactions, and by then sharing his own emotions. "Where is the dignity and respect in asking people about their intimate secrets, when you're not sharing your own?"[169] These conversations help people change their lives.

In organizations and in individuals, conversations about meaning and values need to become explicit in order to facilitate the journey and the return. Ronald Heifetz, director of the Leadership Education Project at Harvard University's John F. Kennedy School of Government, describes what leaders must ask to keep their bearings:

> Which values and operations are so central to our core that if we lose them, we lose ourselves? And which assumptions, investments and businesses are subject to radical change? At the highest level, the work of a leader is to lead conversations about what's essential and what's not.[170]

When the organization's conversations have clearly identified those fundamentals that must never change, it can, by default, assess the vast realms in which everything *is* up for change. Those changes can, in turn, be tolerated because the center will hold. With that understanding clarified, the organization's story is free to become as truthful and compelling as it needs to be. Without that clarity, it will inevitably be a story of confusion, fear and contraction.

In the fall of 2001, Baxter International Inc., a pharmaceuticals company located in Deerfield, Illinois, heard that patients were dying after using their dialysis filters. They immediately recalled the filters and pulled together a team to determine what had happened, while commissioning an independent consultant to do the same. These initial moves were precautionary, since no one had yet proved their filters were at fault. When it became clear that in fact, the filters were implicated in more than fifty deaths, Baxter did not duck the responsibility. It closed down the filter line, shutting two factories, and took a $189 million charge to earnings to cover the costs of closure and settlements with families. The $7.7 billion dollar company publicly accepted responsibility, reporting its actions and their reasons to the Food and Drug Administration and to regulators in countries where the deaths had occurred.

Baxter's president, Harry Kraemer, apologized publicly, even traveling to New York to apologize to the president of one country where twenty-three patients had died. Baxter also reviewed thousands of records of its products and product parts to make sure the faulty processes did not exist anywhere else in its systems. Kraemer's mantra? "Do the right thing."

> I'm not a very smart guy, so let's keep it simple. Think of any problem you need to deal with. There are a million pieces of information that can get involved in a decision. But let's get above the tree line and ask some simple questions. What is the issue? What are the alternatives? What are the pros and cons? What is the best solution? Life is complex, but you can boil the morass down to thinking simply.[171]

Here we see the conversations about what is essential, the values and meaning as they played out in one business story. Strikingly, there has been no long term hit to Baxter's stock, and employees enthusiastically expressed appreciation for the way the situation was handled.[172]

The Same, But Different

One part of the leadership mystery is that the more each of us deeply knows our self, the more we are free to expand it into something less specific, something larger and more universal. When we have self-differentiated in all four domains, when we have come to fully know our central self and its boundaries and limits, then and only then can we freely hold the connection with others that invites them to be their fullest selves. We can offer love with intimacy and high expectations, connection and difference. This allows for the leadership where the people truly say, "We did it ourselves."

In our earlier discussion of the call, clarity and compassion were described as the leader's gifts, gifts both in the sense of abilities and as what leaders offer to the world. Here is a place to which a person clearly returns as the same, but different, whether or not the journey has been externally successful. By deepening the gift of compassion, the caring that drew us out into the world and set us on a leadership journey, we can return infinitely larger. We can return emotionally more mature, more resilient, more capable of love and generativity. We can return morally more mature, more committed to justice and forgiveness. And ultimately, we can return more courageous, more willing to live in and with the anxiety and sorrow, as well as the peace and joy that inevitably accompany commitment.

In our clarity, we can return seeing a far larger and more intricately interwoven world. We can fully recognize current reality and the possibilities inherent in it. We can move intuitively and quickly, responding like a sailor at the tiller to subtle shifts of winds and current, deeply trusting our inner knowing. "This clarity of knowing wells up within us from the central intelligence agency of life itself."[173] We live and are lived by our purpose and our vision. We have become them. We live our story. As Harry Kraemer, who clearly lives his story, noted:

> Ninety-nine percent of people want to do the right thing. I've got 48,000 employees, most of whom care about the environment, or they have parents, or they are parents. I'm representing them. I've got 48,000 people who assume that we're going to do the right thing.[174]

Being a Grownup

Recently, a client told me a story that well illustrates how genuine maturity manifests itself. He had been in a meeting with the director of marketing, who was taking a very unreasonable position, and attempting to torpedo an important project unfairly. My client and his boss, the general manager (GM), made eye contact and instantly decided to take on the marketing director. They did so quite successfully — and pretty brutally. Satisfied with themselves, they left the meeting and returned to their offices.

A half-hour later, my client noticed he was not feeling so pleased with himself or the results of the meeting; in fact, he was feeling almost ill about it. He went to his boss's office, walked in, and said "We screwed up." The GM said, "What do you mean? He deserved it!" My client answered: "You may be right, but we didn't solve the problem, in fact we made it worse *and* we demonstrated really immature behavior in front of our staff that we would never let them get away with." The GM thought for a moment, sighed, and said, "You're right."

At his next staff meeting, my client told his people: "I screwed up. The way I acted in that meeting with the director of marketing was immature and childish and I never should have given in to that impulse." When staff members replied, "But he deserved it!" my client reiterated: "We did not solve the problem, we made it worse. It will be much harder to resolve now. I am committing to you now that I will not ever behave that way with him again. And if I ever see you behaving that badly, you will be in serious trouble. My poor behavior will not excuse yours."

Being mature does not necessarily mean we always behave impeccably. It does mean that we recognize and take ownership when we have not honored our own clarity and/or compassion. It means we publicly own our missteps and continue to set high behavioral standards for ourselves and those around us. That is how we live our story.

Is Death the Destination?

While maturity may be the goal, implicit in the metaphor of journey is the notion of an ending. Jean Vanier comments that "old age is the most precious time of life, the one nearest eternity."[175] Herein lies a critical clue to why we find the conversation about maturity so frightening. Maturity implies aging; aging implies death. If we gain maturity, can death be far behind?

Psychiatrist Erik Erikson's formulation was that the challenge of old age is developing integrity versus succumbing to despair.[176] The well-known author and physician, Rachel Naomi Remen, comments that "in every way but the physical, older is better." What keeps us in Peter Pan's Never-Never Land is the ego's fear of aging and death. People who "age gracefully" keep their integrity intact and revel in the freedom this gives them. Others give in to despair, focus on mourning the loss of their physical capacities and see no joy in what remains. It would seem that in limiting our conversations about leadership maturity today, we have succumbed to despair without ever exploring the possibility of integrity.

We have so few pictures of people who live out their last years in impeccable maturity and integrity, and so many images of people whose rise to the top is followed by increasingly embarrassing and immature behavior. Think for a moment of Jack Welch's desperate over-reaching for one last coup with the attempt to force the European Union into allowing him to buy Honeywell, followed by his marriage-destroying affair with the editor of *Harvard Business Review*. Or Herbert Haft's destroying his marriage and his relationship with his sons in order not to hand over the reins of the Dart Drug/Crown Books business empire his wife and sons had helped him build. Peter Koestenbaum puts it thus:

> We are not conceptually equipped, in our society, to deal with the fundamentals of the soul: death, guilt, anxiety, love, commitment, hope, joy and freedom — our free will. We have lost our sense of myth, the readiness to view the universe as our partner. Therefore, we cannot lead.[177]

In losing that "sense of myth and the readiness to view the universe [the world around us] as our partner," we lose hope, the sense of compelling possibility without which people atrophy or die. We lose, as well, the sense of being in play with forces greater than ourselves, forces with which we can either partner or do battle. We see ourselves instead as either all-powerful or as victims.

We appear also to lose the possibility of a compelling story about mature leadership. We lose the notion of elder statesman, in political or corporate life as well as in family and society. We place into positions of corporate and governmental responsibility person after person who turns out to have lost their moral compass. Then we publicize only these bad examples and sadly wonder, "What went wrong? How is it that our leadership so completely lost its way?"

"Can I be a general manager without becoming an asshole?" one young leader plaintively asked me. The lack of a story about mature leadership, of a clear alternative to being a jerk as a leader, is corrosive, both to young leaders as they seek a way to grow into their best selves as leaders and to our society as a whole.

Growing Toward Arrival

We seek models. In their absence, we need to become those models ourselves.[178] Perhaps, as Robert Kegan points out in his book *In Over Our Heads*, our lengthening life spans allow us to address the possibilities for maturity far more deeply than at any other time in human history. Not that any of us can get it exactly right, but without the conversation about what leadership could and should be, without a living story of leadership that matures, expands and inspires, told widely to ourselves as well as in our communities and our organizations, we will continue to get it mostly wrong.

If we equate maturity only with death, and death with finality instead of mystery, we will continue to avoid maturity. Yet if our stories are to thrive, to achieve greatness, we cannot avoid the reality of the return. To return successfully, one needs a philosophy of life to understand, to use or to target death. As James Hillman, the marvelously crotchety psychologist and author, notes, "It is an enormous mistake to read the phenomena of later life as indications of death rather than as initiations into another way of life."[179]

To paraphrase Hillman, when we fear and neglect those with the most maturity, we fail to recognize that they are the ones who can "shelter civilization from its own predatory frenzy."[180] Having met — and resolved — the monsters on their journey, such elders have gained much in clarity and compassion. In this recognition of the monstrousness within and without, they gain the courage to *be* their wholeness, to become the ones we've been waiting for.

This is ultimately the redemption inherent in the return — that we *can* reject despair for joyful integrity, we *can* regain our child's heart, we *can* integrate our failures, detach from our successes and offer a model of leadership that invites everyone to play and never stops learning. We *can* arrive at a grown-up story about leadership, one that transmutes our passion and pain into love[181] and holds the possibility of being a living story for all of us. When we meet the true elders — a Jimmy Carter, a Warren Buffet, a Frances Hesselbein, an Edward Deming — people who have spent a lifetime speaking the truth and pointing to hope, we find in ourselves renewed energy for our own journeys.

Giving Back

Through our increased awareness, our intellectual and spiritual maturity, we also see a kind of wholeness not available before. As Koestenbaum notes,

> We also discover that the center we reach connects us with the entire universe. To reach that innermost still point is the goal of many religions and philosophies. Once we have found it, we do not feel lonely at all. We feel rich and peaceful. It is the discovery of maturity.[182]

From that center, we see that true leadership "creates certainty by putting us on a path,"[183] not by claiming to monopolize truth. That path becomes synonymous with our leadership story, and the universal living story in which we each play a part. We find ourselves moved to return our gifts in many ways: perhaps by lovingly giving support and encouragement to others, or by publicly expressing gratitude and appreciation, or by celebrating all that has been accomplished, and by a willingness, even a passion, for seeing work taken to the next level.

With such clarity, we can recognize, articulate and enact our stewardship role, our responsibility for the whole, not just the parts. An essential piece of that stewardship is giving back, reaching out a helping hand to those alongside or behind us. Indeed, if clarity and compassion *are* gifts, these gifts can now be passed on. Unfortunately, this frequently does not seem to be the case. In *The Sibling Society*, John Bly acidly notes that many Baby Boomers celebrate their so-called maturity (aka "retirement") with a return to adolescence, hitting the road in their RVs to wander footloose and fancy-free as they did in their teens and twenties. Their bumper stickers proudly read, "I'm spending my child's inheritance."

True leadership elderhood — which is certainly not a function of age, by the way — includes taking an active role in the development of those around us. Whether through coaching, mentoring or otherwise encouraging the gifts, growth and insights of others in the community, or through providing leadership in community activities, part of the return is giving back. Not because it is what one is "supposed" to do, but because it comes naturally from an overflowing heart, a heart that recognizes the many blessings that have come its way and is moved to share them with others.

Having leaders develop leaders is an approach that many organizations seem to have intuitively moved towards. At places like GE and Intel, senior leaders are regularly asked to participate in leadership development with less experienced people in the organization, not only through career development planning, but through conducting training themselves. Some do so out of that overflowing heart, and many do it because it is perceived as politically correct rather than because they have any real grasp of stewardship. They have not yet reached the levels of maturity that would make developing the people around them through their own presence inevitable.

Conclusion: Leading As an Elder

The return operates on many levels, and serves to integrate the whole of the leadership journey that we each take. It is about hearing the call and accepting the reality of that call — that we must each be the hero of our own story. It's about taking the journey. It is about facing the monsters — failure, death, loss and the rest of our deepest fears — and finding the courage to persevere.

Sometimes perseverance is required even after we've returned home, for often the monsters must be faced again. (After monumental struggles to destroy the ring, Frodo must face Saruman, the evil wizard, one more time upon his return home to Bag End in the Tolkien trilogy.[184]) It is about giving back, sharing the fruits of the journey with others.

Ultimately the return is about coming home to ourselves, finding ourselves in a way that enables the sorrow of every ending to be transmuted into the joy of a new beginning, even the final beginning. "One is too full to want, too secure to doubt, too serene to fear."[185] In such maturity, we can freely and fully lead. We have reached elderhood.

SUNLIGHT, HOPE AND HUMAN POSSIBILITY
BILL STRICKLAND OF THE MANCHESTER CRAFTSMEN'S GUILD

William E. Strickland is founder of Manchester Craftsman's Guild in Pittsburgh, Pennsylvania, a remarkable program that combines the arts and training to build successful careers and lives. The program grew from Bill's recognition that the high school teacher who taught him pottery and photography saved him and that he could use the arts to save others.

The result is a beauty-filled training center, designed by Tasso Katselas, a student of Frank Lloyd Wright, that is dedicated to saving peoples' lives. The students are poor and disadvantaged and come from all backgrounds and races. Called the Bidwell Cultural and Arts Training Center, his was the only private program in the city of Pittsburgh that offered training alternatives when the steel industry died in the 1970s.

Taking a highly entrepreneurial approach to the arts and vocational education, Bill has also spun off programs in culinary arts, travel agentry, chemical technology, music recording and orchid growing into successful businesses that train and employ hundreds of people. His model has been so successful that he is being asked to replicate the effort in San Francisco, Denver and Cincinnati.

I have known Bill since high school and have watched him develop from a gangly kid who mostly listened into an extraordinary leader. I put this interview here because he embodies the idea of the return in both senses — embracing death as a mystery and giving back to the community. The conversation with Bill also gave me a different understanding of the call: that for many leaders, it is an aesthetic impulse, a desire to make right and beautiful the world in which they live. He has taken his belief in following where the light takes him — pretty ethereal sounding — and turned it into concrete realities that have helped thousands.

LISA MARSHALL: Bill, I know you have strong beliefs about the power of space and light to affect behavior and about the power of story to help move and motivate people. Tell me, what's your definition of leadership?

WILLIAM E. STRICKLAND: Leadership exists in the area of the imagination and the human spirit. More than anything else it's an attitude, not a set of behaviors. It's an attitude that takes experience, intuition and initiative into account. It's the left and right hemispheres of the brain combined. Leadership consciously and deliberately incorporates a vision of life and a value system. Vision comes as the result of being a good leader, but having vision doesn't mean you're a great leader. The measure of the quality of the vision is what you do with it, not just having it.

LM: What, in your mind, is the internal drive to lead? What is its source?

WES: The source for me is my need to have the world make sense. I'm not satisfied with the way the world is put together. I want to maximize the time I've been given by a higher power to have an impact on this planet that gets it back on balance. I'm connected to the planet; what happens to others has an impact on the quality of my life. When everyone is eating okay, has a warm home and a decent future, then I can have a decent life.

This is not about being a do-gooder. Since I'm someone with an artistic temperament, it irritates me when things aren't organized in an aesthetically pleasing way. Violence, for example, is not aesthetically pleasing. I also understand that inclusion is critical to well-being; people need to be included in society in order to thrive.

My temperament comes from my mother; it had nothing to do with her circumstances and everything to do with her hope. She was someone who was strongly clairvoyant and had a very strong aesthetic.

For example, several years ago, someone gave me an orchid as a gift. I had never seen, or at least paid attention to, orchids before. That first orchid glowed; it had a presence about it. And in that same clairvoyant way, I knew it meant something important.

So I got a book on orchids, and in the back it had the address of the greenhouse that had grown most of the flowers used in the illustrations. I called the guy who ran that greenhouse, Zuma Canyon Orchids, and asked him if I could come visit. He said yes, and so I did. There was an absolutely wonderful light in that greenhouse. And I knew I had to follow that light.

I recognized that part of the solution to my neighborhood was to get flowers into the neighborhood, because their absence is part of what's troubling the people there. So I set out to bring orchid growing to Pittsburgh, to build the greenhouses and train people in my neighborhood to raise and sell them. It was seven years from then to our groundbreaking in October, 2001.

At one point a few years ago, I thought I had this project funded and then we lost the funding. I was bummed. I flew back out to California and reconstituted my energy by watching the sun come up over that greenhouse in Malibu with those beautiful flowers.

Ultimately, leadership is a conversation about vision and values. My values have kept me alive: sunlight, hope and human possibility. I've learned to stay with what I know, to stay on the street, if I want to own this conversation. I follow the aesthetic trail, and turn it into possibility. I convert sentiment into products. I'm driven by a deep aesthetic and by a deep sense of place.

What draws me is the light of Saturday afternoon. I've been following it all my life. It's physical but it's also spiritual. I want that light, the kind you see at a place like Frank Lloyd Wright's Fallingwater, in this neighborhood. And I've known that for a long time. I was right, without knowing why, but I knew what would follow if we got the light here. We would start to have a healthy neighborhood. The light is the big part and then all the things that go to support the light. People tell me I'm pushing in the direction of light; they often tell me that my words do that.

Joe Williams, the jazz musician, told me, "God has picked you, I don't know why and I don't know how, but he's picked you to do this work." Gandhi said: "To lead the people, walk behind them." I left Pittsburgh as a young man to go fly planes and then walked back into this thing, following behind the light.

LM: What was your first experience of, or discovery of, your ability to lead? How has your gift changed over time?

BS: Sitting on my mother's lap, as a little kid, looking at storm clouds gathering one day, I pointed to the clouds and told her that someday I would be there, with the light. I knew then, sitting on her lap, that the feeling would be very powerful and compel me to do things. When I left Pittsburgh, got my pilot's license and started to fly for Braniff, I called and told her, "I got there!" Once I got there, I followed the light here.

There are tests, points along the way where you get it and realize you are a leader. What happened during the building of the Manchester Craftsmen's Center was one. I had a cardboard model, and I walked the streets, carrying that model. I had half the money, and I needed a match, so I got a meeting with the then-governor of Pennsylvania, Dick Thornburgh. It was the first time I really had a powerful validation that I had the ability to lead people. That was twenty-five years ago. Last year, at the University of Pittsburgh's Legacy Laureates dinner, Thornburgh told me, "The most important thing I did as governor was to support you."

LM: How have your gifts matured over time?

WES: I have a respect for these feelings that get generated. I've learned to trust the feelings and act on them, not hesitate. I'm more efficient at recognizing it, less doubtful that it's real. You begin to validate yourself that it's there, that there's a methodology here that's powerful and real. The gift has matured.

And I've figured out the language that makes sense to people; they trust it. I don't know how, but I do know I've learned to do it. The language allows people to trust you, to know that you won't hurt them. Now I don't have to think about the speeches, I see them, like a storyboard. I see the conclusion before I see the beginning, and then I read the audience. Dizzy Gillespie described me as a jazz musician, except people are my instruments, and I improvise constantly.

LM: When do you know you've received the call to leadership?

WES: You answer the call a little bit each day. You become a leader a little bit each day. It's a process of becoming. It's ongoing; I'm still learning how to be a leader. I've studied the people I wanted to be like, learned from how they did things. After I talk, people sometimes come up to me with tears running down their face. I reconnect people with their community.

Jeff Bezos, founder of Amazon, gave us $5 million. I asked him, "Why? Why did you give us all this money?" His answer was "Because you possess something I don't possess — community — and I want to scale it." I don't ever have to change the story. I just speak directly to a person's experience. He's lonely. That's what I speak to.

LM: When do you recognize that in someone else? How?

WES: You see and feel the call in someone else. It's in their language, tone. Then you know you can trust them. By the way they said what they said, you know they won't hurt you. People are looking for safety, security, hope, life and fresh air. There are a lot of people looking for that, looking for a better way to live. There are people who deeply need to be part of a community, and when we take it away from them, they suffer. Those are the ones who get the call. That's also my call, and what I look for in others, and there are people built like that everywhere. I find them; I don't invent them.

LM: What do you as a leader need from others in order to be effective? What roles do you need them to play?

WES: I need enthusiasm. I can make do with everything else. I need to see thoughtfulness conveyed to each other in how we do work together. I find anger painful. I'm thinking about the roles of Darth Vader ... Osama bin Laden. That line between love and hate and light and dark is sometimes very thin. We need to be respectful of that.

LM: Describe your own leadership journey. What do you think is its destination?

WES: I've had to confront my own fear, my fear of being successful. And to recognize that I'm writing the script. As I have succeeded, I have a lot further to fall down; each success means the ante gets higher. As you're much more dependent on yourself, you're that much more dependent on others.

In terms of the destination, I think the way in which you leave is very important. At the moment of my death I want to be able to celebrate the gift that I was given, to leave out of here in a very elegant and understated way. I defeat death by embracing life. I learned that from my mama. I remember visiting Robert Kennedy's grave — there was a tiny cross, nothing else. That was powerful.

I think the closest we get to a destination is to be grateful for the gift we were given, pass it on to the next group and quietly get out of the way. Flight 93 that crashed near Pittsburgh on September 11, now that was class. Faced with your own death, what choices do you make?

LM: What gets in the way of your leadership?

WES: What gets in the way is fear. I've been afraid at times that the stage couldn't support my weight. That at the end of the day, there's something dark about the sun, about the orchids, about the food, about the caring. Now I know better. And I'm not afraid any more. Don't give up on the light. Stay with what got you here. Don't back away.

LM: What are the dilemmas that cause you the greatest concern?

WES: I worry I can't get to all the cities I want to get to, with the time I've got left. Now that I have some of the stuff figured out, I worry I can't make as big a contribution as I'm capable of.

LM: What have been your most transformational experiences as a leader?

WES: Recognizing that my ideas actually work, that I have figured some shit out, and I'm changing people's lives. That has been quite an interesting revelation. My question is: why don't we want to change the planet? Why are we living like this?

LM: What do you understand about leadership now that you didn't five years ago? Ten? How have you evolved or matured?

WES: That you absolutely have to stay with what you know. I don't apologize about the arts anymore; I used to. Now I know the orchids and the sunlight ARE the gig. They're not on the way to the gig. Now my approach is "I'm right; deal with it." I'm prepared to gamble my life for them. As a leader, you put your life on the line.

And I can be content to live with what's inside me; I don't need anything else to be okay. You can live on the sunlight and the flowers and be okay. Once I thought, "If I don't get to that party or get that girl, I'm lost." Now I know better. Arts and aesthetics and hope and memory and flowers keep you alive. I know the flowers will make everything okay at midnight on Friday. That's all I need and I'll be fine.

It surprises you where it comes from. Sometimes you get there when you don't expect it.

EPILOGUE

POSTSCRIPT

We started with a poem. I invite you now to reread it, to discover whether "The Sea" doesn't speak to you, in a different sort of way, of all the things we have explored in this leadership journey. Here it is again, with the phrases that I used as chapter titles italicized:

The pull is so strong we will not believe
the drawing tide is meant for us,
I mean the gift, the sea,
The place *where all the rivers meet.*

Easy to forget,
how the great receiving depth
untamed by what we need
needs only what will flow its way.

Easy to feel so far away
and the body so old
it might not even stand the touch.

But what would that be like
feeling the tide rise
out of the numbness inside
toward the place to which we go
washing over our worries of money,
the illusion of being ahead,
the grief of being behind,
our limbs young
rising from such a depth?

What would that be like
even in this century
driving toward work with the others,
moving down the roads

among the thousands swimming upstream,
as if *growing toward arrival,*
feeling the *currents of the great desire,*
carry time toward tomorrow?

Tomorrow seen today, for itself,
the sea *where all the rivers meet,* unbound,
unbroken for a thousand miles, the surface
of a great silence, the movement of a moment
left completely to itself, to find ourselves adrift,
safe in our unknowing, our very own,
our great tide, our great receiving, our

wordless, fiery, unspoken,
hardly remembered, *gift of true longing.*

~ DAVID WHYTE[186]

We also started with a story, so we shall end by returning to that story. It is, of course, a living story, so all we can do is bring the reader up-to-date and imagine another chapter, speculating on what wants and needs to happen.

The process of interviewing and writing has been a profound one for me. Of course, it led me to learn a lot about what growing up/maturing looks, sounds and feels like, in all four domains. And to reflect on how very, very far I still have to go! At the same time, events in the world, in business, in our faith communities and in international affairs continue to deepen my conviction that the absence of a conversation about leadership maturity and about elderhood is costing us dearly.

Writing has also been an experience in facing my own monsters. Summoning the courage to go public with what I have known for a long time — that great, grown-up leadership and love are inextricably intertwined — was not an easy step. In fact, I ducked it completely in the first draft, and it took the loving and critical eye of several of my manuscript readers to get me to own it. I know all too well what a radical message this is in the communities I serve.

It's fortunate that it takes time to write books, because then authors have a chance to do some of their own development along the way. In my case, I have had opportunities to look hard at the leadership I've provided in my own life. Some of what I saw I liked; some, I didn't. Summoning the focus and discipline to keep driving the book forward in the face of family and business obligations at times took every bit of resolve that I had. My "warrior archetype" had a good workout during this process! In the end, I'm profoundly grateful for the experience — for the learning and for the deep and loving support I had along the way.

~   ~   ~

So, I imagine that in the first few months after the book is published, there won't be a lot of reaction, beyond the limited numbers of people who have heard about the book and will buy a copy. (Some of whom then buy copies to send to friends.) Then perhaps I'll hear — second-hand — that, using the conversation-starter guide in the appendix, some executives in a global company have started a series of company-wide explorations of their leadership maturity. As a result, they ultimately find themselves challenging a lot of the promotion practices in the company and deliberately encouraging leadership, rather than just rewarding good management practices. In the process, they discover they are rewriting the company's story.

A colleague and I have already begun to develop a self-assessment tool that offers a yardstick for leaders in those four domains of maturity — intellectual, emotional, moral and spiritual. I imagine we continue to have a good time developing it and testing it, and that people who use it seem gratified by the results. We make it available online, and people want to have conversations about the results. The resulting online discussions further our thinking considerably.

A little later, I hear about an urban non-profit director who asked her board of directors to read the book, and then requested a conversation with them about why she was not getting real leadership from them. It starts a deep dialogue that leads to significant recrafting of the organization's story and a renewed sense of vitality.

Slowly, other conversations are reported: a forum for CEOs in a Midwestern city that uses the book to ask themselves what kind of leadership they are providing, both inside and outside their organizations; a business school that puts the book in their leadership curriculum. Someone contacts me about developing some tools for measuring leadership maturity in the four domains at an organizational level.

A group of young engineers in a large high-tech organization begin, on their own, to use the idea of maturity in the four domains as part of their annual rating and ranking process. They claim that it produces better results. I even get inquiries about translating the book's ideas into other languages, including some tribal languages, with new ways of describing elderhood developing as a result.

True success, however, comes a few years later, when I begin to see other leadership maturity models being proposed in the business journals, as well as in some of the education schools. Lively and thoughtful conversations begin to show up in lots of places, not just in places where management or leadership issues are usually discussed. I even hear a couple of stories of community organizing institutes being contacted by corporate human resource departments trying to figure out how to develop the kind of "egoless" leadership they have read about in various places.

As I hear them, I work hard on sharing these stories widely, setting up a website for that purpose. I know they will help to amplify a growing awareness that elderhood is something that can be aspired to and sustained, not as an end-point, but as an ongoing journey of exploration, growth and wonder. I know the leadership journey will continue, that people's thinking about and understanding of leadership maturity is far from complete.

I begin to see that leadership's story is changing and growing. It is now offering possibilities for a future in which "regular" people begin to see themselves as leaders of their own lives. The story now tells of a world in which ordinary people consistently discover themselves to be creative, compassionate, competent and courageous, *because their leaders see and encourage those qualities in them.*

The story tells of a world in which leaders — all of us — lead by sharing the stories that really matter and opening our hearts to each other in the process. We don't scapegoat, we don't blame and we're not afraid to admit when we don't know all the answers. These stories are visible in our media, not just told amongst ourselves. It is becoming a world in which leaders consistently speak the truth and point to hope.

~   ~   ~

Then I know I've accomplished what I set out to do.

THE END, FOR NOW ...
          ... OR, THE BEGINNING.

ACKNOWLEDGEMENTS TO MY MERRY MANY

Beyond the teachers listed at the beginning, I have had the best of companions on this journey. I give great thanks for and to:

* **Larry Wolken,** my hero, spousal unit and lifetime companion extraordinaire, master of technical support and the rock on whom I rest;

* **Ginger** and **Melissa Wolken Marshall,** my most wondrous productions ever, who gave me insight, support and encouragement all along the journey and good company to boot;

* **Rebecca Beauman,** Queen caregiver, Mistress of my schedule, Organizer of my life and Controller of every bloomin' detail in this process from start to end, who reads my mind and makes it happen;

* **Bob Guldin, Nancy Hughes, Vicki McCown** and **Johanna Pino,** proofreaders, editors and book designer, who are the reasons this book reads and looks as well as it does;

* **Sheila Resnick,** counselor and wise woman, who saw that in writing this book, I was honoring my heritage, and **Alice Marshall,** my mother, whose foresight gave me the gift of a place in which to write and whose genes gave me the insights from which I write;

* **Barbara Glacel, Lew Hyde, Susan Kanaan, Sy Kaufman, Karen Lam, Dianne & Laurie Marshall, Cindy Phillips, Fiona Quinn, Ken Scharf, Dave Tyrrell, Alan Venable** and **Caroline Wood** — purveyors of synchronistic support, one and

all, who offered just the right book to read, right story to add, right bit of support or right suggestion to think about at just the right moment to point me back to the path and keep me on my journey;

• My fellow Smart Workers and especially my colleagues in the concenter Alliance — **Charles Feltman, Dee Kinder, Karen Bading, Janet Crawford** and **Larry Solow** — fine minds and gallant souls who have supported, provoked, challenged and nurtured my thinking, my learning, my doing and my being throughout the journey of this book.

All errors of omission or commission are mine, and should not be confused with any of the contributions of my merry many.

APPENDIX A:
TEN-STEP GUIDE FOR EXPLORING
MATURE LEADERSHIP

A prime purpose of this book is to get conversations going about leadership, most specifically about the idea of leadership maturity. In service of that goal, here is a guide to help get such conversations started. It is only a guide; feel free to innovate and make it work for you.

1) **Find a partner.** Two heads are better than one. Get someone else whose opinions you respect (which is not the same as agree with) to read the book. Play with some of the questions that follow or whatever else develops in a couple of conversations. If the conversation is stimulating enough, gather a group for regular discussions. If you ask eight to ten people, you'll probably get four to eight who show up for any given conversation. You and your partner can guide together. Pick a venue: it could be informal, like a brown bag lunch series, or a formal part of regular staff meetings. It could even be part of or all of an off-site retreat.

2) **Decide on the initial format for conversations.** This doesn't mean it's the format you'll end up with, but it gives people a starting point. Some people will want to use the book as the structure, and read a chapter or two for each session. Others would rather just work off the list of questions that follows. You may want to focus the conversations on your own organization or part of the organization, or you may want to keep it more generic. All of these work — you just need to put some structure in place so the group knows what to expect. And it's fine if it changes over time.

3) **Understand your role.** As a leadership maturity conversation guide, you are consciously accepting a unique role — and developmental opportunity. While you probably would not have convened these conversations if you didn't have a strong point of view, your goal is also to get other people thinking hard about these issues for themselves. The way to do that is by asking more questions than giving answers. The reasons for this are:

a) Consciously or otherwise, people grant power to the opinions of the designated "leaders." The purpose of these conversations is to get everyone involved in thinking for themselves. When you ask questions that get other people thinking, the whole group gets involved more quickly. Keep in the mind that, as the questioner/guide, you shape the dialogue enormously.

b) If the role of grownup leadership is to get others to freely enroll, great questions are one of the key tools in your toolkit. People always more fully own the understandings they've reached themselves. This will give you a great opportunity to practice your questioning/shaping skills.

c) When the guide mostly asks questions, it helps shorten or sidestep some of the group dynamics that may otherwise derail the conversation. (More on that next.)

4) **Be aware of group dynamics.** You may be lucky and have a terrific conversation the very first time, but normally it takes a little while for groups to cohere. People have to sort themselves out vis-à-vis one another before they can fully attend to the purpose at hand. Remember the lesson from Bruce Tuckman in your team dynamics class — "form, storm, norm, perform" — the stages EVERY group will go through? Here are some moves you can make to move the group through those stages so that you can quickly settle down to some really juicy conversations.

FORM. This is the stage where everyone is figuring out who everyone else is in this context. It helps if you *tell/remind everyone of the reasons they are meeting* (set a clear context), and ask each person to introduce themselves in some appropriate way, including what they want to get out of their participation. Capture those goals, and refer back to them periodically as the conversations proceed, e.g., "Joe, I know when we started you said you were particularly interested in knowing more about how to develop yourself as a mature leader. Are you getting what you need along those lines, or should we focus on that subject a bit more today?"

STORM. This is where "who has the power in this group and how will I be treated?" is raised. It can take the form of people actively pushing for power or withdrawing to let the dust settle. Your goal is to get the group to own that power AS A GROUP as soon as possible. Do this by asking them to *set norms immediately*. The purpose of the norms is to answer the issues of who has power and how people will be treated. Some useful norms include:

- Deciding on roles — convener, time-keeper, note-taker (if desired), gate-keeper, etc. — and whether they are they permanent or rotating,
- Honoring time commitments,
- Deciding whether or not it is okay to interrupt one another,
- Honoring confidentiality — "what's said here stays here,"
- Staying in inquiry mode, rather than moving into advocacy, and
- Asking group members not to create any agreements to which they can't honestly commit.

At the same time, don't treat infractions as crimes. Instead, use them as opportunities to have additional conversations about leadership maturity. (This, by the way, helps keep people from focusing on your power as the issue.) For example: "We set a norm about being on time +/- five minutes, but I've noticed we keep starting about 15 minutes late. What domain does this behavior fall into? What does it tell us about ourselves? Do we want to do anything about it?"

NORM. Here's when the group resolves the power issues and begins to step up to owning the power. As guides, *be willing to actively ask that the group honor its norms for the first few meetings.* After that, you should start to see others taking on that responsibility. (If not, you need to check if the group is still stuck in storming, and figure out some moves for "unsticking" them, such as asking people to rotate the responsibility.) You'll notice the quality of the conversations will markedly increase when the group gets to this stage.

PERFORM. Now there is real momentum for the conversations, and *you're playing less and less of a guiding role.* If you find yourself wanting/needing to move away from questioning and just contribute your own point of view and assertions, it is easy to do so at this point.

5) **Know what conversation you are in.** Is it a conversation for history, a conversation for possibility or a conversation for action? For the most part, the leadership maturity conversations will be conversations for history — how it came to be that things are the way they are — and conversations for possibility — how do we want them to be? At some point, however, you will want to shift into conversations for action: making commitments to do specific things differently in the future. It's important to be clear when that happens. If some

people think you're still in a conversation for possibilities, and others think they switched to a conversation for action, you can build up a lot of frustration fast.

When you have had more than one kind of conversation in a session, it can be helpful to end with a round of commitments or next steps. Ask people to say what actions they are personally committed to taking, and by when. If there are group actions, be sure that each group member has individually agreed. In both cases, a written record follow-up can be very useful.

6) **Know who you're in conversation with.** Who are the big picture thinkers? Who needs to build the big picture up out of all the details? Watch for communication breakdowns between them — it's very hard for the detail-oriented folks to figure how the big-picture people get where they do, and it can make them quite testy. Similarly, who are your extroverts and who are your introverts? The introverts can participate much more fully if there's a clear agenda ahead of time, or if they at least know what questions are going to be discussed.

Extroverts, on the other hand, won't really be able to know what they think until they've had a chance to talk for a bit. Sometimes you need to remind the introverts, who wouldn't dream of saying something until they'd thought it out, that the first thing extroverts say is probably not what they actually think — that they have to talk to figure out what they think. As guide, you want to make space for all kinds of thinkers. That means sometimes letting people talk as they will and sometimes inviting comments or giving everyone a chance to respond to a question or comment before conversation resumes.

7) **Don't be afraid of silence.** In our results-driven world, silence is usually assumed to be a waste of time. That's not true in

these conversations. The questions that go into exploring leadership maturity are not trivial: they lead to some pretty serious thinking, and potentially some deep sharing. Give it time and space to happen. If you're finding that pauses make you nervous, make yourself count slowly to ten before you jump in to try and jumpstart the conversation. You'll be surprised at how much richer the conversations can get when people don't feel like they're constantly competing for airtime.

8) **Choose carefully the kinds of questions you use;** they drive the quality of the conversation. You already know that you need to be asking open-ended questions that allow for exploration, rather than closed questions that merely elicit a "yes" or "no" response. Beyond that, there are three levels of questions to design:

   a) Level 1 — what the book says. Make sure people have a shared understanding of the points the book is making before they start to debate them.

   b) Level 2 — what the book means. This is where you start to explore: "So if she says this, does it mean xx under these circumstances?" Here the goal is to explore, to reach common understanding of the implications of what's being discussed.

   > NOTE: Level 1 and Level 2 are likely to show up in the same conversation; that's fine, and you may have to clarify which is which in order to keep the conversation clear.

   c) Level 3 — assessments, thoughts and opinions. Here's where you take your shared understandings and extrapolate forward. For example: "Well, if that's what emotional maturity is, how well do you think this organization is doing?" Or, (and here's where you might move to a conversation for action) "If we are ever to see ourselves mature in this area, what kinds of things do we need to be doing differently?"

9) **Pay attention to the kinds of answers you get.** it is important to distinguish between facts and opinions. We call statements of fact "assertions." They can be validated by others or through research. We call opinions "assessments." They are the conclusions we draw from our facts, and can represent both our wisdom and our blind spots. The clearer we are about these distinctions, the higher the quality of our conversation.

Unfortunately, most of us tend to merge the two, and then assume that our interpretations of the facts represent reality. As guide, you will often find you have to pry the two gently apart in order for people to comprehend and appreciate what one another is saying. Peter Senge's concept of balancing inquiry and advocacy by articulating the assumptions and data (assessments and assertions) that underlie a given conclusion can be a helpful discipline for the group to develop.

10) **Share what you've learned.** We would very much like to hear what worked and what didn't, as well as the outcomes of these conversations. To that end, we've set up a website at www.LeadershipMaturity.com where you can post stories, share learnings and be in conversation with other Leadership Maturity Conversation Guides. We are particularly interested in the questions that developed during your conversations. Please share any new questions that you created or that evolved from the group's conversation. Join us there!

QUESTIONS FOR LEADERSHIP MATURITY CONVERSATIONS

Preparation

1) What is your personal definition of a leader? What are the characteristics of that person? Develop a "leader's job description." Name some leaders in today's world. Discuss how they fit your characteristics for leadership.

2) What story or stories are dominant in your life and/or your organization right now? Are they compelling to you? Why?

3) Does the telling of the story have to be verbal? Can it be situational? Can it be acted out? How can it be told "over and over," in many different ways so that it is embedded in the organization? What might those ways be?

4) What stories does your organization hold about the nature of leadership? Are they stories you believe?

The Call

5) When do you know something is actually a "call"? How do you know a call should be listened to? How does it manifest itself in you? In those close to you? In leaders you admire?

6) What do you think the source of the call is for most people? Is it a gift? What are some examples of clarity or compassion in calls you have seen?

The Hero/Leader

7) What's the difference in your mind between being a hero and a leader? Are they synonymous? Must you be both, or is one a step on the way to the other?

8) Should leadership be a solitary journey? Is that even possible? Who should go along? Contrast Peter Pan and Nelson Mandela (or the mature leader of your choice). Who went with them? What is the difference in their leadership from a follower's perspective?

The Journey

9) Does the hero always complete the journey? Is she a failure if she doesn't? Can she pass off her leadership role to other potential leaders along the way? Is the breakdown or failure most likely to be one of the monsters? Internal? External? For what reasons?

10) Would you describe your organization's culture as autonomy-focused, connection-focused or balanced? How would you describe yourself in terms of the autonomy/connection balance? If they are significantly different, what are the consequences of that? What are the benefits and costs of being in that position?

The Monsters

11) In what domain do you think you personally face the most monsters? Name them. In what domains do you think your organization faces the most monsters? Name them. Which are

the worst? Are the personal and organizational monsters different? How should they be addressed?

12) Describe a difficult situation your organization currently faces. What are the monsters in that scenario? Imagine that you represent intellectual, emotional, moral and spiritual wisdom. Give your organization advice about how to handle those monsters from each of the four domains.

Metamorphosis

13) Did you ever have a "wormhole" experience? Do you know others who did? What happened? What triggered it? What was the end result? What changed? For better or worse?

14) Are you prepared to accept your leadership role in the organization? Can you let go of doing everything yourself? Are you ready and willing to live under the microscope? Can you live with or function with not having answers?

The Return

15) Describe maturity:

   a) For yourself.

   b) For your boss

   c) For your organization

   d) For your country.

16) As a leader, whether in your own life or in an organization, what truths do you think you speak? What hope do you point to? Are there things you stop yourself from saying or hoping?

17) To what would you like to return at the end of your current leadership journey? To whom? What would you like to give back?

18) Write your own living leadership story in 4-5 paragraphs. Then write a paragraph or two that tells where you would like the story to go next. Read these stories to one another and comment in this format:

   a) What I appreciated about this story was…

   b) What I learned from this story was…

   c) What I still wonder about this story is…

19) What is your one big hope for yourself and for this organization? What are the new conversations that will help us achieve this hope?

20) Based on our conversations, what needs to change in this organization? How do we want it to be? Where are we now? What do we need to do more of, better or differently in order to get there?

21) Based on our conversations, what commitments need to be made in order to change? (Remembering that the only person you can change is yourself.) By whom and by when? Are we willing to make them? What competing commitments do we hold that might derail us?

22) If modeling, *being* the change you want to see, is the most powerful form of influencing others to change, what changes

in your own behavior can you publicly commit to or ask to be held accountable for? Who, within your own sphere of influence, do you hope to impact by such changes? How will they know you have changed? How will you know they have changed?

APPENDIX B: LEADERSHIP CONVERSATION QUESTIONS

These questions are designed to explore your thinking through a very specific lens, that of the leadership story or the hero's journey. Thus, we will explore how you have experienced a call to leadership in yourself and others, the roles others play in your leadership, what your leadership journey has been like, what issues you have faced, the ways in which you have changed and the ways in which you have stayed the same.

1) What is your definition of leadership?

2) What, in your mind, *is* the internal drive to lead? Describe it. What is its source? Is it related to immediate others, to a larger vision, etc.?

3) What was your first experience of, or discovery of, your ability to lead? How has your gift changed over time?

4) When do you know you've received the call to leadership? When do you recognize it in someone else? How? How do you know the call has been answered?

5) What do you as a leader need from others in order to be effective? What roles do you need them to play?

6) Describe your own leadership journey.

7) What gets in the way of your leadership? What are the dilemmas that cause you the greatest concern?

8) What have been your most transformational experiences as a leader?

9) What do you understand about leadership now that you didn't five years ago? Ten? How have you evolved or matured? How haven't you?

APPENDIX C:
CONVERSATION CONTACTS

ROBERT DILTS
Chief Scientist
Isvor Dilts Leadership Systems
P.O. Box 67448
Scotts Valley, CA 95067
Phone: (831) 438- 8314
Fax: (831) 438-8571
robert@IsvorDilts.com, rdilts@nlpu.com
www.IsvorDilts.com, www.nlpu.com

VADM JOSEPH W. DYER, US NAVY (RETIRED)
VP/GM Defense
iRobot
DyerJoseph@aol.com
www.iRobot.com

DARYA FUNCHES, EdD
President/CEO
REAP™ Consulting
179 Thomas Road
Mossyrock, WA 98564
Phone: (360) 983-8628
Fax: (360) 983-8648
reapconsulting@myhome.net

RICHARD STROZZI-HECKLER, PHD
President
Strozzi Institute
4101 Middle Two Rock Road
Petaluma, CA 94952
Phone: (707) 778-6505
Fax: (707) 778-0306
Richard@StrozziInstitute.com
www.StrozziInstitute.com

JULIO OLALLA
President
The Newfield Network
2804 Fountain Grove Terrace
Olney, MD 20832
Phone: (301) 570-6680
www.NewfieldNetwork.com

WILLIAM E. STRICKLAND, JR.
President/CEO
Manchester Bidwell Corporation
1815 Metropolitan Street
Pittsburgh, PA 15233
Phone: (412) 323-4000 x102
Fax: (412) 321-2120
wstricklandjr@mcg-btc.org
www.ManchesterGuild.org
www.Bidwell-Training.org

BARBARA WAUGH, PHD
Co-founder, e-inclusion
Hewlett-Packard
1501 Page Mill Road
Palo Alto, CA 94304
Phone: (650) 857-2273
Fax: (650) 858-1862
Barbara.Waugh@hp.com
www.BarbWaugh.com

MARGARET WHEATLEY
President
The Berkana Institute
P.O. Box 1407
Provo, UT 84603
Phone: (801) 377-2996
info@berkana.org
www.MargaretWheatley.com

LISA J. MARSHALL
Principal
The Smart Work Company
Phone: (202) 829-0795
Fax: (202) 829-5324
lisa@LeadershipMaturity.com
www.LeadershipMaturity.com
www.SmartWorkCo.com

ENDNOTES AND REFERENCES

The Sea

1 David Whyte, "The Sea," *Where Many Rivers Meet* (Langley, Washington: Many Rivers Press, 1990, 1998), 9-10.

Preface

2 Joseph Campbell, *The Power of Myth* (New York, New York: Doubleday, 1998), 123.

3 Edwin H. Friedman, *A Failure of Nerve: Leadership in the Age of the Quick Fix*, ed. Edward W. Beal and Margaret M. Treadwell (Bethesda, Maryland: The Edwin Friedman Estate, 1999), 7.

4 Friedman, 13.

5 Friedman, 71.

6 M.W. Watts, ed., *Cross Cultural Perspectives on Youth and Violence* (New York, New York: Elsevier, 1998).

7 Carol J. Loomis, "I Own This Problem," *Fortune*, 3 February 2003.

The Who of Leadership: Preparation

8 Mary Parker Follett, "XXV: Neighborhood Organization vs. Party Organization: Leaders or Bosses," *The New State* (University Park, Pennsylvania: Pennsylvania State University Press, 1998), 227.

9 John W. Gardner, *Living, Leading and the American Dream* (San Francisco, California: Jossey-Bass, 2003), 155.

10 David Tyrrell, conversation with author, 31 October 2001.

11 Rayona Sharpnak, conversation with author, 25 June, 2002.

12 Robert Dilts, conversation with author, 28 March 2002.

13 Charles Fishman, "One Man's Drive, One Company's Courage," *Fast Company* (June 2003): 122.

14 Gordon Shaw, Robert Brown and Philip Bromiley. "Strategic Stories: How 3M is Rewriting Business Planning," *Harvard Business Review* (May 1998): 42.

15 David Gaster, "A Framework for Visionary Leadership," in *New Traditions in Business: Spirit and Leadership in the 21st Century*, ed. John Renesch (San Francisco, California: Berrett-Koehler Publishing, 1992), 170.

[16] Rachel Sahlman, "Clara Barton," *SPECTRUM Home & School Network* (accessed 23 August 2003); available from http://www.incwell.com/Biographies/Barton.html; internet.

Why Stories?

[17] Barry Lopez, *Crow and Weasel*, (New York, New York: Farrar, Straus & Giroux, 1990), 60.

[18] William H. Calvin, "The Emergence of Intelligence," *Scientific American* (October 1994): 103.

[19] Shaw, 42.

[20] Jeanie Daniel Duck, *The Change Monster* (New York, New York: Three Rivers Press, 2002), 143.

[21] Arie de Geus, *The Living Company* (Boston, Massachusetts: Harvard Business School Press, 2002), 11.

[22] Thomas Stewart, "The Cunning Plots of Leadership," *Fortune*, 7 September 1998, 165.

[23] Richard Strozzi-Heckler, conversation with author, 11 December 2001.

[24] Richard T. Pascale, *Managing on the Edge* (New York, New York: Touchstone Books, 1990), Chapter 6 and a story told by Jim McNeil, former UAW plant leader.

[25] Brenda Zimmerman, personal communication, June 1990.

[26] Howard Gardner, *Leading Minds*, (New York, New York: Basic Books, 1996), 49.

[27] Ron Brade, NASA CLG Member, 2002.

[28] Thanks to Karen Bading, Fernando Flores and Julio Olalla for these ideas.

Leadership's Story

[29] Seamus Heaney, ed., *Beowulf: A New Verse Translation*, (New York, New York: W.W. Norton & Company, 1999), 3.

[30] Wilfred Drath, *The Deep Blue Sea: Rethinking the Source of Leadership* (San Francisco, California: Jossey-Bass, 2001), 39.

[31] Drath, 65-66.

[32] This concept of including and transcending previous stages is found in many of Ken Wilber's writings.

[33] David Whyte, *The Heart Aroused: Poetry and the Preservation of the Soul in Corporate America* (New York, New York: Currency/Doubleday, 1996), 164.

[34] Drath, 87.

[35] Hoshin is a Japanese Total Quality Management (TQM) approach that helps organizations build consensus, focus efforts and achieve results.

[36] Drath, 87.

[37] Drath, 159.

[38] Drath, 160.

[39] William M. Isaacs, *The Dialogue Project Annual Report*, 1993-94, 18-19.

[40] Isaacs, 18-19.

[41] "The Caring Company," review of *Corporate Culture and Performance*, by John Kotter and James Haskett, *The Economist*, 6 June 1992, 75.

[42] Jean Vanier, *Community and Growth* (Mahwah, New Jersey: Paulist Press, 2001), 221.

[43] Bill Moyers, *A World of Ideas II: Public Opinions from Private Citizens* (New York, New York: Doubleday, 1990), 144.

[44] Joseph Jaworski, *Synchronicity*, (San Francisco, California: Berrett-Koehler, 1998), 66.

[45] Carol Stoneburner, conversation with author, 22 April 2002.

[46] Henry D. Thoreau, *The Essays of Henry D. Thoreau*, ed. Lewis Hyde (New York, New York: North Point Press, 2002), ix.

[47] Thoreau, xvi.

[48] Thoreau, xv.

[49] David Whyte, *Crossing the Unknown Sea: Work as a Pilgrimage of Identity*, (New York, New York: Riverhead Books, 2002), 47.

[50] Whyte, *Crossing the Unknown Sea*, 47.

[51] Rosamund Stone Zander and Benjamin Zander, *The Art of Possibility: Transforming Professional and Personal Life* (Boston, Massachusetts: Harvard Business School Press, 2000), 81.

[52] Noury Al-Khaledy, conversation with author, 15 October 2001.

[53] Curtis Sittenfeld, "Hope is Weapon," *Fast Company* (February 1999): 178.

[54] Fari Amini, Richard Lannon and Thomas Lewis, *A General Theory of Love* (New York, New York: Vintage Books, 2001), 144.

[55] Jim Collins, *Good To Great* (San Francisco, California: Harper Collins, 2001), 62.

[56] Vanier, 91.

[57] Peter Perl, "Hallowed Ground," *Washington Post Magazine*, 12 May 2002, 32-47.

The Gift of True Longing: The Call to Action

[58] "Moria," *The Lord of the Rings: The Fellowship of the Ring*, DVD, directed by Peter Jackson (Los Angeles, California: New Line Home Entertainment, 2002).

[59] Whyte, "The Sea," 9-10.

[60] Whyte, "The Sea," 9-10.

[61] Serge F. Kowalski, "His Brother's Keeper," *Washington Post Magazine*, 15 July 2001, 17.

[62] Jim Collins, "Level Five Leadership," *Harvard Business Review* (January 2001): 70.

[63] Brian Dumaine, "Donald Petersen: A Humble Hero Drives Ford to the Top," *Fortune*, 4 January 1988, 23.

[64] Robert K. Greenleaf, *Servant Leadership: A Journey into the Nature of Legitimate Power and Greatness* (Mahwah, New Jersey: Paulist Press, 2002), 15.

[65] Frederick Buechner, *Wishful Thinking: A Theological ABC* (San Francisco, California: Harper Collins, 1993), 119.

[66] Whyte, "The Sea," 9-10.

[67] Daniel Goleman, *Working With Emotional Intelligence* (New York, New York: Bantam Doubleday Dell Publishing Group, 2000), 106.

[68] Goleman, 187.

[69] Whyte, "The Sea," 9-10.

[70] Greenleaf, 22.

[71] Amini, et al, 63.

[72] Greenleaf, 21.

[73] John A. Byrne, "How to Lead Now: Getting Extraordinary Performance When You Can't Pay for it," *Fast Company* (August 2003): 64.

[74] Amini, et al, 64.

[75] Byrne, 69.

Rising From Such a Depth: Being the Hero in Our Own Story

[76] Margaret Mark and Carol S. Pearson, *The Hero and the Outlaw: Harnessing the Power of Archetypes to Create a Winning Brand* (New York: McGraw Hill Trade, 2002), 103.

[77] "The Leader and Leadership: What the Leader Must Be, Know, and Do," *U.S. Army FM22-100*, 9.

[78] Author unknown.

[79] Amini, et al, 85.

80 Greg Ip, The Outlook, "Tech Bust: What Goes Around, Comes Around," *The Wall Street Journal,* 16 July 2001.

81 Mark Shipman, comments on draft manuscript to author, December 2002.

82 Tyrrell, conversation with author.

83 Heaney, xv-xvi.

84 Heaney, 46.

85 Sir Walter Scott, *Rob Roy* (New York, New York: Signet Classic, 1995), 418-419.

86 Office of the Assistant Secretary of Defense for Force Management Policy, "Active Component Enlisted Applicants and Accessions," *Population Representation in the Military Services: FY 2000* (November 2001): 2-23.

87 The United States military has given much thought to the issues of leadership and leadership development, and I do not in any way mean to belittle their substantial insights. It is in the inevitable nature of any organization in which people leave after three years that messages about the deeper issues of character and moral development, ones the military has in fact thought through quite thoroughly, are not deeply embedded in the average soldier. Witness the Tail Hook scandal.

88 Ron & Susan Zemke, "Where Do Leaders Come From?," *Training Magazine* (August 2001): 44.

89 Carol Beckwith & Angela Fisher, "Masai Passage to Manhood," *National Geographic* (September 1999): 65.

90 Robert K. Greenleaf, *Servant as Leader* (Indianapolis, Indiana: Robert K. Greenleaf Center, 1982).

The Currents of the Great Desire: The Pull of the Pit

91 Campbell, 41.

92 de Geus, 11.

93 William Bridges, *Managing Transitions: Making the Most of Change* (New York, New York: Perseus Publishing, 2003), 5.

94 Friedman, 29.

95 Jim Messerschmitt, conversation with author, 7 March 2002.

96 "Bill Rauch: Theater of Action," *Leadership for a Changing World, 2001* (accessed 6 October 2003); available from http://leadershipforchange.org/awardees/awardee.php3?ID=27; internet.

97 "Liz Lerman," *The MacArthur Fellows Program,* http://www.macfound.org/programs/fel/fel_overview.htm.

[98] Jeffrey Pfeffer and Robert I. Sutton, *The Knowing-Doing Gap: How Smart Companies Turn Knowledge into Action* (Boston, Massachusetts: Harvard Business School Press, 2000).

[99] I am indebted to my colleague Chuck Appleby for this concept of the "wormhole."

[100] Lawrence H. Ford and Thomas A. Roman, "Negative Energy, Wormholes and Warp Drive," *Scientific American* (January 2000): 49.

[101] Mort Meyerson, "Everything I Thought I Knew About Leadership Is Wrong" *Fast Company* (April/May 1996): 71.

Untamed by What We Need: The Nature of Monsters and How We Meet Them

[102] Goleman, 74.

[103] Bernardo Carlucci, *Shyness: A Bold New Approach* (New York, New York: Perennial Press, 1999), 90.

[104] Nancy K. Dess, "Tend and Befriend," *Psychology Today* (September/October 2000).

[105] David Dorsey, "Andy Pearson Finds Love," *Fast Company* (August 2001): 85.

[106] Dorsey, 84.

[107] Dorsey, 85.

[108] Dorsey, 86.

[109] Gene Krantz, Project World keynote, May 1996.

[110] Joe Dyer, conversation with author, 19 March 2002.

[111] Hara Estroff Marano, "The Depression Suite," *Psychology Today* (May/June 2003): 60.

[112] Robert Kegan, *The Evolving Self* (Boston, Massachusetts: Harvard University Press, 1983), 107.

[113] Bridges, 5.

[114] Kegan, *The Evolving Self*, 131.

[115] Kegan, *The Evolving Self*, 83.

[116] Kegan, *The Evolving Self*, 114.

[117] Carol S. Pearson, *Awakening the Heroes Within: Twelve Archetypes to Help Us Find Ourselves and Transform Our World* (San Francisco, California: Harper Collins, 1991), 126.

[118] Pearson, 128.

[119] Carol Dweck, "Believing in Fixed Social Traits: Impact on Social Coping," in *Self-Theories: Their Role in Motivation, Personality, and Development* (Philadelphia, Pennsylvania: Psychology Press, 2000).

120 Dan Schulman, "How We Perceive Self-Deception," *Psychology Today* (May/June 2003): 15.

121 Pearson, 127-128.

Feeling the Tide Rise: Facing Our Monsters

122 Julio Olalla, conversation with author, 21 March 2002.

123 Goleman, 41-42.

124 Dyer, conversation with author.

125 Dyer, conversation with author.

126 Goleman, 41.

127 James Fowler, *Stages of Faith: The Psychology of Human Development* (San Francisco, California: Harper Collins, 1995), 80.

128 Fowler, 85.

129 Kegan, *In Over Our Heads*, 231.

130 Richard Conniff, "Rethinking Primate Aggression," *Smithsonian Magazine* (August 2003): 62.

131 Fowler, 82.

132 Fowler, 83.

133 Fowler, 84.

134 Peter Goodman, "Sherron Watkins: The Woman Behind the Whistle-Blower," *Business Woman Magazine* (Fall 2002): 29.

135 Goodman, 32.

136 Edward O. Wilson, "The Biological Basis of Morality," *The Atlantic Monthly* (April 1998): 70.

137 Fowler, 274.

138 Fowler, 200-201.

139 Barbara Waugh, conversation with author, 9 January 2002.

140 Fowler, 211.

141 Marc Gunther, "Tree Huggers, Soy Lovers and Profits," *Fortune*, 23 June 2003, 99.

142 Richard Norton Smith, *Patriarch: George Washington and the New American Nation* (New York, New York: Houghton Mifflin Company, 1993), 19.

143 Polly Labarre, "Do You Have the Will to Lead?," *Fast Company* (March 2000): 228.

144 Labarre, 228.

145 Waugh, conversation with author.

146 Jack Stack, *The Great Game of Business* (New York, New York: Currency Doubleday, 1994).

[147] Darya Funches, "The Inner Experience of Transformation: A Study in the Use of Self as an Instrument," Unpublished Dissertation (Amherst, Massachusetts: University of Massachusetts), 1994.

[148] Darya Funches, "Three Gifts of the Organization Development Practitioner," in *Emerging Practice of Organization Development*, ed. Walter Sikes, Allan Drexler and Jack Gant (Alexandria, Virginia and San Diego, California: NTL Institute and University Associates), 1989.

Growing Toward Arrival: Wormholes and Metamorphosis

[149] Dave Kelly, conversation with author, 13 December 2001.

[150] Tyrrell, conversation with author.

[151] Drawn from David Whyte, Keynote Speech, International Coach Federation, 1999.

[152] Lucius Theus, conversation with author, 15 December 2001.

[153] Kate Sweetman, "Embracing Uncertainty," *MIT Sloan Management Review* (Fall 2001): 8.

[154] Kegan, *In Over Our Heads*, 334.

[155] Kegan, *In Over Our Heads*, 351.

[156] Labarre, 230.

[157] Labarre, 230.

[158] Labarre, 230.

[159] Labarre, 230.

[160] Dilts, conversation with author.

[161] "Public Policy: George Lee Butler," *The Heinz Awards, 2002* (accessed 13 October 2003); available from http://www.heinzawards.net/recipients.asp?action=detail&recipientID=67; internet.

[162] Collins, "Level 5 Leadership," 67.

[163] Darya Funches, conversation with author, 6 March 02.

[164] Pearson, 12.

Where All the Rivers Meet: The Return

[165] Parker Palmer, *The Courage to Teach: Exploring the Inner Landscape of a Teacher's Life*, (Indianapolis, Indiana: Jossey-Bass, 1997), 58.

[166] Palmer, 58.

[167] Robert Rabbin, *Invisible Leadership: Igniting the Soul at Work* (Lakewood, Colorado: Acropolis Books, 1998), 208.

[168] Pamela Kruger, "A Leader's Journey," *Fast Company* (June 1999): 126.

[169] Kruger, 126.

170 William C. Taylor, "The Leader of the Future," *Fast Company* (June 1999): 134.

171 Keith H. Hammonds, "Harry Kraemer's Moment of Truth," *Fast Company* (November 2002): 96.

172 Hammonds, 96.

173 Rabbin, 208.

174 Hammonds, 98.

175 Vanier, 140.

176 Fowler, 211.

177 Peter Koestenbaum, *Leadership: The Inner Side of Greatness* (San Francisco, California: Jossey-Bass, 1991), 212.

178 Gaster, 170. Gaster was himself a leader in the development of leadership coaching, and his early death a great loss to all who are thoughtful about leadership.

179 Hillman, 60.

180 Hillman, 190.

181 Kathy Bauer Braglia, conversation with author, 5 February 2002.

182 Koestenbaum, 198.

183 Koestenbaum, 198.

184 Tony Deady, conversation with author, 8 December 2002.

185 Rabbin, 159.

Postscript

186 Whyte, "The Sea," 9-10. Italics added.

PERMISSIONS